WIN WITH YOUR
CUSTOMER

Devendra

Chennai • Bangalore

CLEVER FOX PUBLISHING
Chennai, India

Published by CLEVER FOX PUBLISHING 2023
Copyright © Devendra 2023

All Rights Reserved.
ISBN: 978-93-56483-82-8

This book has been published with all reasonable efforts taken to make the material error-free after the consent of the author. No part of this book shall be used, reproduced in any manner whatsoever without written permission from the author, except in the case of brief quotations embodied in critical articles and reviews.

The Author of this book is solely responsible and liable for its content including but not limited to the views, representations, descriptions, statements, information, opinions and references ["Content"]. The Content of this book shall not constitute or be construed or deemed to reflect the opinion or expression of the Publisher or Editor. Neither the Publisher nor Editor endorse or approve the Content of this book or guarantee the reliability, accuracy or completeness of the Content published herein and do not make any representations or warranties of any kind, express or implied, including but not limited to the implied warranties of merchantability, fitness for a particular purpose. The Publisher and Editor shall not be liable whatsoever for any errors, omissions, whether such errors or omissions result from negligence, accident, or any other cause or claims for loss or damages of any kind, including without limitation, indirect or consequential loss or damage arising out of use, inability to use, or about the reliability, accuracy or sufficiency of the information contained in this book.

Acknowledgments

I am grateful to the almighty for giving me the courage, strength, and blessings to share my experience through this book. I thank the owners and leaders of the organization where I work for nurturing a customer-focused culture as their core value. Exposure to this culture has given me opportunities to understand and work on all aspects of the customer's journey. I thank the Confederation of Indian Industries (CII) for bringing frameworks such as EFQM and Customer Obsession to India. Practicing these frameworks has helped me immensely professionally. With the blessing of my parents and the support of my dear friends and colleagues, I could implement many learnings in my own life. I thank Godrej Construction (A Strategic Business Unit of Godrej & Boyce Mfg. Co. Ltd.) – The winner of the CII-EXIM Award for Business Excellence year 2021 and 2022, for allowing me to share their practices in this book.

Writing this book was not possible without the motivation, support, and push from my wife, Amrita, and my mentor, Mitesh Khatri and they deserve all the credit for this attainment. I am sure that this book will bring an abundance of success to all readers and their customers alike.

Index

Chapter 1. Does a Winning Customer Make You a Winner? 1

Chapter 2. What Customers Want 11

Chapter 3. What Customers Get 33

Chapter 4. Balancing Want & Get 49

Chapter 5. How Much to Communicate 79

Chapter 6. Keeping Them Interested 97

Chapter 7. Ahead of Competition 113

Chapter 8. Winning Together 132

Chapter 9. Conclusion 160

Readers' Tasks...*165*

Answer to Quiz..*169*

References...*170*

About Author *171*

Chapter 1

Does a Winning Customer Make You a Winner?

In today's era, you will hardly find a person unfamiliar with the word *'customer.'* This includes the person selling diamond jewellery or a luxurious car, as well as the person delivering newspapers to your house every day. Not only people around us are familiar with this word, but they chant it now more often than before. Today, if you go to a local street shop and find the shop unattended, you will naturally ask the neighbouring shopkeeper about it.

The most expected response will be a call from him to the missing shopkeeper saying, "Please come fast, a customer is waiting for you."

A sense of urgency and concern for the customer's time will be there. Even, when the shopkeeper comes back, a basic apology is expected most of the time. So, there is an increased sense of customer focus all around, though it may vary from city to city. Metropolitan cities like Mumbai, Delhi, Chennai, etc. will have better customer service than a tier 3 or tier 4 city. Even today, in my hometown, I find many shopkeepers shutting their shops between 1 to 4 PM for lunch, followed by an afternoon nap. There is nothing wrong with having a peaceful nap and I have no complaints about this. The problem comes when you want something urgently, but this nap shatters your dreams of having it on time.

Confidence goes further down when you get the message, "Namaskar! The mobile number you are trying to reach is currently switched off. Please try again later."

Let us try to understand why this happens. Does this person not want to sell? Does this person not want to make money? Has this person attained Nirvana? Does he not want to grow the business? Does this person not dream of becoming Ambani or Adani?

To me, all these reasons are not the main cause in the majority of cases. The main cause is that the business owners are not aligned to support their customers in what they are wanting to achieve. Let me explain. When someone books a flight from one place to another, they want to reach their destination on time. When they reach, they will have their further plans to be executed. Someone may have a business meeting with a prospective

Chapter 1 Does a Winning Customer Make You a Winner?

business partner or need to attend to a medical emergency or catch a connecting international flight, and so on.

Thus, the airline needs to align itself in a manner that supports the customers in what they are wanting to achieve. In the above example, all passengers would like to reach their destination on time, and that is why they avail of airline services. Now, do you think the airline would be able to do this if they nap like our dear shopkeepers? No! Absolutely not. They must be on their toes to ensure the flight departs and lands as per the schedule.

What happens when an airline ably supports customers again and again? Yes, the customer would achieve whatever he/she wants. Can I safely say that when customers consistently achieve what they were expecting, they are the winners? They are winning with the support of the airline. They may not say that a deal is struck, or their dear ones are saved because of the airline, but they will register the airline's performance in their subconscious mind. And when they travel the next time, their experience and subconscious mind will lead them to prefer the same airline. It may be that due to other factors like timing and cost, the customer will not use the same airline again. But if, in case, the other airline gets delayed for some reason, the customer will register this as well. At times, the reason for the delay may be technical and beyond the control of the airline. But the majority of the customers will not give leeway for that. Next time, if they must choose between these two airlines, they will lean towards the first airline. When this happens, the chosen airline acquires a loyal customer. A loyal customer means repeated business and more importantly, recommendation through word of mouth. Whenever someone speaks to this loyal customer about their travel plans, he or she is bound to share their own experience and the chosen airline has a higher chance of getting this booking as well.

In fact, think about this; if I ask you to recommend an airline for my travel, which airline will you recommend? Just give this a minute.

If you have already decided on a name for me, I will ask you to internally realize why have you recommended this name. According to me, the reason for you to give a name will either be one of the following:

i) Your own good experience (on time, service, cost, safety, etc) with the airline
ii) Your not-so-good experience with the closest alternative or competitor of the recommended airline
iii) A testimony for the airline by your friend, relative, or colleague
iv) General market perception about the airline you have through newspapers, websites, reports, TV channels, etc.

Chapter 1 Does a Winning Customer Make You a Winner?

So now, a first-time customer like me chooses the recommended airline and this airline continues to perform and support the new customer to achieve what he wanted to and make him feel like a winner. Is it not obvious that the new customer will get converted into a loyal customer and the chain reaction will continue? So, in addition to the airline's own marketing and sales strategies, this parallel network marketing will continue to work on its own, thereby giving more business to the airline.

Can someone deny that while supporting the customer's win(s), the airline will also be more efficient as their ground time will reduce and air time will increase? If the airline continues its journey like this, it is going to be a winner for sure. This approach is what I call the **"Win With Your Customer" approach.**

Well, adopting this approach of "Win With Your Customer" is easier said than done. There are many aspects and nuances one should understand to achieve this status. I will be detailing these aspects one by one in the further chapters of this book. This book aims to give businesses (no matter big or small), professionals and individuals a lens to see the **customer as a partner in their success**. We will go through simple and practical methods which can be adopted by the readers of this book in their area of influence.

Are you ready for this journey? I am sure you are.

Let us start with the most important thing–**mindset.**

For a very long time, we have seen customers and sellers seated at opposite sides of the table. In this scenario, it is assumed that if customers gain something, it will be at the cost of the sellers and vice versa. Almost at all stages of their association, negotiations take place and various techniques of negotiation are used by both sides. Moreover, people are hardwired to negotiate to the point of breaking. This ensures that the best is achieved by their side. However, if one side feels that they have lost during the initial stage of negotiation, they will seek opportunities to get ahead of the other side during further stages. Many times, this game goes on and on and the situation comes to a point of no return. This creates a bad experience for the seller and customer alike. We have seen many big deals and associations getting cancelled and even reaching a court of law.

Thus, there is a need to change this perspective completely. Let me take this customer-seller relationship to a higher level. For a moment, let us assume that the seller is not merely a seller because his role seems to be just selling his product or service, taking the agreed money and exiting. The story is over. What if we start changing the seller's role into a **provider**? A provider is an entity or person providing support to the next entity or person (customer)

Chapter 1 Does a Winning Customer Make You a Winner?

for achieving something which is directly consumed by them or taken ahead further to support the next entity or person (customer's customer). By following this approach, the provider (seller) will need to think of the ultimate consumer and the goal which he is supporting. This will bring true alignment and purpose for the provider (seller). The provider now thinks more about the ultimate user and understands his own role in this supply chain.

In the example of the airline, the airport operator takes charges from the airlines for using the airport, its infrastructure and other services. This makes the operator a seller and the airlines a customer. Now, if the operator does not see himself as a support provider to the airline, it will be difficult for the airline to serve its customers the way they desire. For example, the aircraft may reach the airport on time but due to inadequate infrastructure or technical support, the flight landing may get delayed.

So, how do we bring this change? Like I mentioned, the most important and first thing to address is the mindset. To change the mindset of an organization, the first person who needs to take the plunge is **the topmost leader**. In the case of a private or small entity, the responsibility comes to the owner or founder of the entity. Until there is a complete belief in leadership about "Win with Your Customer," they will not move towards this. And in absence of leadership's conviction, the sheep will graze without the shepherd on this turf and most likely will be directionless.

Let me give you an instance from my own experience. I joined my company in 2005 and after some time was given the role of handling customer complaints. I had done construction engineering during higher education and as you may know that they do not teach any subject related to customer focus in engineering. With this background, it was difficult to handle customer service and accept the fact that customers can actually ask for better service. Moreover, if a customer got angry about something, I used to get even angrier. I was not able to accept that a customer can even point out something inferior in our product or in the manner I handled the complaint. I used to try everything in my control to prove to my seniors that there was nothing wrong with my service handling and that all the problems were with the customers. Fortunately, my leaders and the organization themselves are known for their focus on quality and customer-centricity.

Some of the issues went up to our then COO (Chief Operating Officer), who shared his surname and many behavioural traits with 'Father of the Nation,' Mahatma Gandhi. One day, he called me into his office as he knew that I am the person on the ground and was not handling the situation with the right mindset. He asked me to outline the problems I was facing while handling customer complaints. I told him what I felt, and he patiently listened to everything, asking a few questions in between.

After I finished, he told me to relax and started writing on the whiteboard in the room.

A few minutes later he told me, "Dhikra! (Parsi word for Son) Whenever you are handling customer matters, always remember the golden rules I have written for you here. If you follow these rules, you will grow in your life, both professionally and personally."

The rules were -

Rule 1: The customer is always right!

Rule 2: If the customer is ever wrong, refer to rule number 1.

This was something unimaginable at that time and I was surprised that my COO is telling me something like this. Later, I realized that it is easy to learn new things, but it is quite difficult to unlearn. And to learn customer-centricity, I had to unlearn my biases. By giving me these rules, my Guru, my COO was helping me come out of my own biases.

This great leader not only changed my team's and my mindset through his words but he also led by example.

He visited unhappy customers with us, interacted with them, cleared the miscommunication, and amicably resolved the issues. During his leadership, he influenced senior and junior team members alike and created an atmosphere where customer concerns were treated with utmost care and empathy. He set the right direction for the organization and nurtured a highly customer-focused culture within the team. This culture is now deep-rooted and the company enjoys high customer affinity and best-in-industry customer feedback. He is not with us anymore but his words of wisdom and guidance are alive in many people's way of working including mine.

Therefore, the bottom line is that the first step towards adopting the "Win With Your Customer" approach is to change the mindset starting from the leaders. Hence, if you are the leader or influencer in your organization or firm, you have taken a step in the right direction by reading this book. And if you are not, then find a way to bring them on board for "**Winning With Your Customer Faster.**"

I will talk about more things that the leadership and other team members can do to bring cultural change in subsequent chapters.

Chapter 2

What Customers Want

Would life not be very easy if we could know what the customers want? All of us, directly or indirectly, serve a customer as part of our jobs. We also hear about unsatisfactory customers often. Even the best of the organizations will find some customers who are not happy with them, if not grossly unsatisfied. Logically, the simplest solution to this would be to know what customers want and provide them with the same.

But is it really that easy to know what the customers want? Do all the customers think and behave in the same manner? Does a customer react in the same manner to the same service at different points in time? Does the customer's mood affect his behavior? To me, these questions do not have one right answer. Let us take a simple case to start with. Imagine a mother providing food for her family. In a way, she is a provider (seller) to the family who consumes the food (end user or the customer of the product). By the way, let us not bring any undue emotions here, I am trying to give an analogy. So, coming back to the lady of the house. There is a husband, in-laws and 2 young kids in the family. She must cater to the different needs of the family in aspects such as:

i) Time-based preferences - Kids need breakfast at 7:30 AM, in-laws need it at 8:30 AM and husband at 09:00 AM. Therefore, in case she wants to serve hot Bhajiya (Deep fried Indian snack) to all the consumers she will have to stretch the kitchen timing from 06:30 AM to 09:30 AM.

ii) Type-based preferences – The kids and in-laws prefer a light breakfast, whereas the husband prefers a heavy breakfast. Taste and liking preferences are a topic in themselves.

iii) Routine-based needs - If the husband goes to the gym for an hour and burns some calories, he will have the right to retake those. Therefore, a proper nutritious meal will be required.

There are many more factors that the lady of the house must take care of. Needless to say, out of her love and affection towards the family, she tries to provide meals to suit all preferences of the family members. But is it possible for her to keep everyone happy all the time? Very difficult. Someone or the other may not like what is being offered. But in the end, out of respect for each other's choices and liking, they may accept what is being cooked. It may be a compromise but is worth doing.

Chapter 2 What Customers Want

Now, let us run this analogy to a restaurant setup. The same family goes to the restaurant. Each one will order what they want and in whichever sequence they want. Here, the chef cannot expect that the family will be all right with whatever is being served to them. In case a dish is not tasting as expected, they may return it. They may also choose to finish the meal but not to repeat the dish in the future or the restaurant itself for that matter. Recommendation to a friend is unlikely.

Therefore, the point I am driving here is that in a professional environment in today's era, **customers are unwilling to compromise.** This is despite different expectations and requirements for the same product. Today, customers are spoilt for choice. One cannot say that I will make my product or service the way I want and the same should be used as-it-is by all my customers. We all know that India and the rest of the world have moved from a **"seller's market" to a "buyer's market"** long ago. The levels of service have gone up substantially. So, why should a customer compromise? Now, in this scenario, what should the provider (seller) do to be better in business?

The challenge is complex but solvable. The trick is to take a systematic approach. While you read this book, together, we will attempt to develop this approach for you. I am sure that you as an individual or a business will benefit from this. However, you will have to participate sincerely and wholeheartedly. If you use your actual data and experiences for the methods I am suggesting, the approach will automatically be tailor-made to your needs. To simplify the methods, I will split them into tasks and I request the readers to do the tasks as we move along the chapters.

Let us start.

Task 1: Take a fresh notebook or an MS Office File (Word or PowerPoint) and use the same as your journal for all the tasks. A physical copy is preferred but if you want to create a digital copy, please feel free to do the same.

On top of the first page of the notebook write, "I believe and follow two Golden Rules."

After this write the golden rules I mentioned in Chapter 1 in a large font:

"Rule 1: The customer is always right!

Rule 2: If the customer is ever wrong, refer to rule number 1."

Coming back to knowing what customers want. To understand this better we will break the answer into two parts. First, we will understand—**who our customer is** and second, **what they want.**

Who is our customer? Obviously, the one who opts for our product or service is the customer. However, to be successful in business we must know customer details and behavior to the best of our ability and as minutely as possible. To do the same, we need to categorize customers.

Let us categorize them in broader heads to start with. The heads will be the factors on which customers are different from each other. Generally, this categorization is done by sellers unknowingly as part of the routine business. The more experience a seller has, the better the understanding of the categories. The categories differ from business to business but many of them can be common as well. A few categories, which can be used, are explained below.

A. Demography-based

This is the very first and basic category. Here, the bifurcation happens based on age, gender, income, education, profession, marital status, etc. You would have observed that almost every new enquiry form requires you to share these details with the provider. Companies having B2C (business to customer—where the product or service is offered to individual customers) business collect and use this information for various purposes. For example, take an apparel shop offering clothing for the entire family. It needs to understand the fashion sense of young college kids, the functional needs of the elderly, and the comfort needed for a toddler. Another example is a company selling residential flats. Here, it would need to align flat prices as per the income capacity of its prospective clients. The layout of the flat offered will also be aligned with the age and family status (married or single, joint or nuclear, etc.). There are numerous examples where providers (sellers) design their products to cater to demographically categorized customers.

It is also important to understand that these or other categories explained ahead may not be overly important for every business or professional. For example, a company selling a mobile SIM card does not need to worry too much about the age, gender, or marital status of its customers. Although it is a different matter that when they move towards a higher level of customer categorization (segmentation) these details will also become important. Because demographic changes may impact customer behavior and thus, the company may have to offer different tariff packages.

As readers, you must understand the applicability and relevance of the categories to your product and service. As a progressive step, readers need to first realize and address the core applicable categories and then go to secondary applicable categories. A robust new product development approach should consider both primary and secondary applicable categories. I will touch upon new product development in chapters 6 and 7. The forthcoming **task** will help you to identify primary and secondary categories for yourself with ease.

B. Geography-based

This category is simply segmenting customers based on their country, state, city, town, etc. An important category for a business having its presence in different locations. Changes in the weather, language, habits, and customs due to changes in customer location are important factors to know about. For example, the type of warm clothes customers will prefer in the UK versus UAE will differ drastically. A company selling insurance products will need to categorize customers into urban and rural because in urban areas life-term insurance may be a successful product whereas in rural areas crop or vehicle insurance might do better.

A higher level of geography-based categorization will be to identify the geographic location of your customer. For example, assume you have two shops in the same metropolitan city, say Mumbai. One shop is in Ghatkopar (predominantly consists of Gujarati communities) and the other is in Kurla (predominantly consists of North Indian communities). You will realize that the majority of the customers as well as their buying patterns will differ in these two areas. Even for a shop located in a neutral place, categorizing the customers as per their city or state of origin will help in knowing what product will sell better.

C. Association-based

Under this category, customers can be differentiated based on the type of association they have with us: first-time buyers, repeat customers, loyal customers, etc. This is an important category for an operational strategy. For example, a doctor realizes that out of his 100 patients, only 5-8% are first-time visitors. This may be good for him at present. However, it also indicates that in the long term, the flow of patients will become stagnant. In that case, the doctor needs to focus on his marketing or promotional methods. In the reverse scenario, when most of the patients, say 80%, are coming for the first time for consultation, the promotional methods are working fine but it is possible that the quality of treatment or the patient experience needs to be worked upon. Other than the reasons I mentioned, there can be various factors because of which the ratio between first-time, repeat, and loyal customers may change. An important point is to realize that this bifurcation and its analysis can help professionals or businesses decide where they need to work upon.

D. Product or service-based

Generally, this category is useful for businesses that offer distinct types of products or services to their customers. For example, Reliance will segment customers of Reliance retail and Reliance capital separately. Ideally, if the product or service is very distinct, it should be considered as a separate line of business (LoB), and the customers of each LoB should be categorized and addressed uniquely. However, when the scale of the business is smaller and the key team handling the entire business is common, the categorization will be useful.

Now that we have seen four key customer categorizations (segmentations), let us find out which are applicable in your area of work. Doing the right customer segmentation is a key fundamental premise of "Win With Your Customer." You will find that a customer's requirements and behaviours change across the categories. To know what a customer wants, knowing why they would want anything is a crucial factor. Categorization will help us know 'why' better. Therefore, let us do Task 2.

Task 2: **Now,** with your experience and explanation of the categories, please fill in the below table for your business or profession. While doing so you may, in addition, consider the product or service which you intend to launch in the future as well. Mark the categories or subcategories which directly influence the behavior of your customers or future customers as **primary (P)**. Mark the categories or subcategories which may influence a few customers, or indirectly influence customer behavior as **secondary (S)**. You can mark the remaining fields as **not applicable (NA)**. Depending on your business model and size, you can choose to do categorization at the overall business level or the line of business level or the product or service level. For first-timers, I will suggest doing one quick round for whatever level you feel is easy. But have a clear understanding that as our journey goes forward, this categorization may need to be done again. **This process is ever-evolving and we should be open to completely discarding our own past work.**

Task 2: **Working table** (users can customize this table as per applicability).

Legend: Primary - P, Secondary - S, Not Applicable - NA

Sr.	Category	Applicability/Relevance		
		For LoB/ Product 1	For LoB/ Product 2	For LoB/ Product 3
A	**Demography-based**			
	Age			
	Gender			
	Income			
	Education			
	Profession			

Continued...

	Marital status			
B.	**Geography-based**			
	Country			
	State			
	Urban/Rural			
	Language/Culture			
	Environment			
C	**Association-based**			
	First-time Buyer			
	Repeat Customer			
	Loyal Customer			
D	**Product/Service-based**	**(Applicable if the table is used at LoB / overall business level)**		
	_____			
	_____			
E.	**Other Business-Specific Category**			
	_____			
	_____			

Task 3 (Working table): This task will be a continuation of the mapping you have done under task 2. Here, take each LoB/product one by one and identify the different customer groups under the applicable subcategories.

The primary subcategories should be taken first. Let me explain with one example for a general practitioner (doctor offering medical services). For a doctor, the primarily applicable subcategory under demography will be the age of the patients, education, and gender. Income will be secondary whereas marital status and profession may not be applicable. In addition, medical field service-specific subcategories will be applicable.

Below is a working table filled in for the example of a doctor:

For the LoB/Product (e.g. doctor)		
Primary Subcategory	**Customer Groups Under Subcategory**	**Reason for Grouping**
Age	• Infant • Kids (5-17) • Adults (18-50) • Senior (50+)	Medication and treatment will be different for each group. The level of acceptance for treatment may also be different.
Treatment needed	• Routine check-up • Common illness • Emergency • Specialization	Qualification, experience and infrastructure for offering the treatment will be different. Response time will also differ.

Chapter 2 What Customers Want

Here is another filled-in example for a B2B (business to business) service provider. I am taking a construction company that takes contracts from various developers/builders. Let us do task 2 for this company followed by task 3.

Sr.	Category	Applicability/Relevance for Construction Contracting Business
A	**Demography-based**	Not applicable as they deal with other companies (Developer/ Builder)
B.	**Geography-based**	
	Country	NA as it operates in only India
	State	Primary (as they are in multiple states)
	Urban/Rural	Secondary (open to work as per contract)
	Language/Culture	Secondary (applicable for operational issues during construction. Not applicable from a direct customer point of view)
	Environment	Secondary (applicable for working conditions and working methodologies)
C.	**Association-based**	
	First-time Buyer	Primary (new contracts from new clients)

Continued...

	Repeat Customer	Primary (new contract from an existing client)
	Loyal Customer	Primary (assured business from an existing client)
D	**Product/Service-based**	
	Turn-key Projects	Primary
	Labour contract only	Primary
	Hybrid contract (labour + material + free issue material)	Primary
E.	**Other Business-specific Category**	
	Residential Projects	Primary (As the company is an expert in this field)
	Commercial Projects	Secondary (As the company is not an expert but can do this work)
	Infrastructure Projects	NA (As the company does not want to go into this space)

Let us prepare the customer group for key primary categories for this company (task 3 illustration) –

Chapter 2 What Customers Want

Primary Subcategory	Customer Groups Under Subcategory	Reason for Grouping
First-time Buyer	• Aspirational Client • New Entrant	Aspirational Client is a must-have due to various reasons such as good paymaster, big brand, high future potential, better standards, the opportunity to learn, etc. Whereas more research is needed for a new entrant. Risk is to be assessed better. Their expectations may be different than industry.
Repeat Customer	• Preferable Client • Less Preferable Client	Based on experience and future business potential, experience in payment history, adherence to commitments, working relations, value alignment, etc. become key factors.

Continued...

| Residential Projects | • High Rise & Iconic Projects
• Mid & Low Rise
• Mass Housing | Required skills, competency, and set of employees/labours might be different for different customer groups. The profit margins and other financials will be different for different groups and will impact decision-making to either bid or not bid for a particular project. |

As per the above examples please do task 2 and task 3 for your business/profession.

What the Customer Wants

Now that we have understood our customer categorization better, let us explore what they want. We discussed in the first chapter that when a customer chooses any product or service, they want to achieve something. This achievement is the basic use of the product and a key driver for customers to take it. This core function customer is looking for is his '**Need.**'

Do you remember a scene from the hit Bollywood movie *3 Idiots* where Aamir Khan hides the Rolex wristwatch that Kareena's fiancé (Suhas) purchases for her? Aamir tells Suhas that Kareena has lost the watch. Suhas gets restless when Aamir says, "It's ok, purchase a new one for her."

Suhas says, "What are you saying man, it was worth Rs. 4 Lakhs."

Aamir exclaims, "4 Lakhs!! Mine is Rs.250 and it shows the same time." Here, Aamir is saying his need for the watch is to check the time. Whereas Suhas's need for the watch is more of a status symbol. Suppose you are in the business of selling Watches, will it not be important for you to understand what **needs** your customer wants to address through your product? It is absolutely important. Now, imagine a scenario where you have not categorized your customers properly and have no clue how many Aamirs and how many Suhases come to your shop in a month. What type and range of products will you keep in your shop? Whereas after demographic categorization under task 2, if you realize that 90% of your customers are the type of Aamir, you can keep the entire range of basic watches. From a business point of view, you may also realize that 90% of your customers are purchasing low-margin items. To earn your targeted amount, you will have to sell more watches. To sell more watches you need to attract more customers and thus, specific marketing efforts will be needed.

Therefore, the question is, if you categorize your customers and understand their needs, will you be able to make customers feel delighted?

The answer is – You will be able to offer what customers need, but there is no guarantee that customers will take it. Why so? Because when we address only customer Needs, we are supporting the basic function. Customers may achieve what they want to, but **how** they want to achieve is yet to be fulfilled.

As a watch seller, if I offer a watch worth 4 Lakhs to Suhas without a brand, it is meeting his need. But will he want to spend 4 Lakhs rupees and be in a position where only he knows that he is wearing an expensive watch? No, he would like the brand he is wearing to be associated with an image of an expensive brand. The design and the look have to be unique and as per the latest fashion trend. The watch should not require any service for a long time and even when needed, service has to be of top class. He may want to be treated in a very diligent manner at the showroom. He will imagine the showroom to be nicely designed and maintained. This 'how' part is nothing but customers' **'Expectations.'** How a customer wants or expects the product or service to be delivered, performed, or maintained is his expectation. The expectations are generally not explicitly spoken by the customers and each organization addresses them differently. Successful organizations not only fulfill the needs but also the expectations of customers.

Different customer groups can have different expectations for the same product. Let us take the example of a mobile phone. Generally, a working person on the field will expect the mobile to have a good battery backup so that it can work without any interruption. Whereas a homemaker may expect the camera to be of very good quality rather than being too concerned about battery. But both of them may have the same budget for the mobile purchase. All successful mobile companies know this. They not only micro-categorize their probable customers but also do research in detail about the needs and expectations of each of the micro-categories. That is the reason you will find so many models of mobile phones being available and continuing to be launched routinely within similar price ranges.

Taking the cue from successful businesses, let us attempt to map the need and expectations of your customers under **task 4**. You will need the outcome of tasks 2 & 3 for doing task 4 properly.

Task 4: From the task 3 table, we will take each **customer group** and identify their needs and expectations. Let me explain by continuing the doctor's example. You may similarly complete Task 4 for your business/profession in this format.

Task 4: Working table with an example of medical service.

Customer Groups	Needs	Expectations
Infant	Get appropriate treatment	Parents of infants will expect delicate and hygienic handling. Doctors should identify the root cause quickly as kids can't explain. The effect should be seen immediately.
Kids (5–17)		With less speaking, doctors should understand more since patients don't want to sit in the waiting area with others for long.
Adults (18–50)		A proper explanation of illness, logic, and reasoning is needed. The doctor's diagnosis should match what one read online. Appointment-taking should be easy and match patients' office hours
Senior (50+)		The doctor should listen to my issue with patience. The place should have seating and a washroom facility. A less crowded clinic that is close to the home is preferred.

Continued...

Chapter 2 What Customers Want

Routine check-up	Preventive check-up	Reliable and good quality testing. Maximum coverage of checking at a lesser cost. Appointment at a convenient time. Some loyalty programs by the clinic will be welcome.
Common illness	Get appropriate treatment	Fast diagnostic and quick relief treatment. Follow-up visits should not be needed. Treatment without tests is preferred.
Emergency	Life-saving responses and treatment	Customers will prefer a proper hospital and avoid individuals practicing G.P. This group may not come here except for first aid/Response.

At the end of this task, you would have already realized some misalignment in what you generally do for customers v/s what their needs and expectations are. If you realize that there is some mismatch, let me assure you that you are on the right track. Identifying a problem is the first step towards solving it and in further chapters, I will elaborate on how to treat this misalignment.

Summing up Chapter 2, to know what customers want we need to:

A. Know who our customers are:

Broad Categorization

Subcategories with relevance (Primary and Secondary)

Groups under the subcategories

B. Know what customers want:

What they want to achieve (need)

How they want to achieve (expectations)

Chapter 3

What Customers Get

In the previous chapter, we tried to understand what customers would like to have. An equally important area is to know what customers get and experience in reality. Without knowing this, it will be very difficult for us to be on the customers' side. To understand this better, I will narrate a few situations, which you would have faced yourself in life. While reading these situations, I would like you to remember how you felt in such situations. In case you have not encountered these situations yourself just imagine that you are going through the same now.

Imagine that after a lot of research and years of planning, you have booked an apartment from a developer in your city. The cost of the apartment is 2 Crores. You are self-funding it for 50 Lakhs and have taken a loan of 1.5 Crore. You are paying the EMI of 1.5 Lakhs a month and are currently residing in a nearby rented apartment for a monthly rental of 50K. The developer had promised to complete the apartment in 4 years. You had planned to expand your family once you shift to the new house as you will be able to balance your finances once rental expenses go down. However, the building is not complete even after 6 years. Every time you reach out to the developer, he gives different technical reasons like material is not available or labour has vanished from the site or there is some notice from government authorities, etc. Not only is your planning on a personal front getting affected but you are also strained financially because the rent goes up by 10% every year and the bank has also revised the interest rate.

You take legal advice and are told to file a case against the developer. After initial hassles, you file a case and find out that either you have to wait for the project to get over or you can get your money back with basic interest and penalty. You are not able to exit from the deal as the value of property in the vicinity has gone up tremendously in the last 6 years. Ultimately, you will have to settle for an apartment in some other area with the money you are getting refunded. Anyone will feel helpless and frustrated in this scenario due to the **developer not meeting the originally promised timeline.**

In another situation, imagine you have planned a family trip to Rajasthan. With a good amount of online research, you shortlist a palace hotel. It is situated close to the desert and has fantastic pictures on the online booking platform. The price is fairly decent and the stay looks exciting. When you reach the hotel, the infrastructure, garden, location, and interiors all look similar to the pictures on the website. The entire family is happy. After a few hours, you go to the hotel pool and realize that the pool is deep and only adults can use it, so kids are out. Still, you manage to enjoy the pool but when the towels are provided, they are smelling of an overdose of fabric spray. When you go to your room and use the bathroom, you encounter a foul smell. On talking to the staff, they say a line is choked up and they offer an alternate room. In the new room, the toilet is fine but one of the walls gives away the secret of past leakage. Despite being in a tourist-friendly location, the hotel does not offer any cultural or entertainment programs. It does not have any place where kids can have indoor activities. There is no provision for visiting nearby sand dunes. The buffet dinner and breakfast are very delicious but do not offer any Rajasthani delicacies. So, at an overall level, the stay experience becomes average from the expected excellent. This happened because the hotel **service did not fulfill your unsaid expectations.**

In another situation, imagine you own a factory that manufactures bicycles. The core metal components are produced in-house and you depend on your suppliers for other parts like tyres and seats. You are expecting huge demand during the upcoming festive season which is a first after a pandemic. Your order book is quite promising. You inform your suppliers about this requirement and they assure you of their full support. However, there is some delay from the seat supplier. You contact him and he says that due to a machine breakdown, his supply is delayed. He assures you that he will speed up his production and though a little delayed, the order will be delivered. You believe him and continue your production. However, after some time your final dispatch is getting affected because of the non-delivery of the seats. You decide to visit the supplier and find out more information. You get shocked to see that his production is fully on. In fact, there are additional people put on the job than usual. On further investigation, you get to know that the supplier has taken orders from other purchasers as well and it is beyond his capacity to fulfill all of them. As he is getting paid more by them, he is prioritizing those orders. This makes you feel cheated as the supplier **has knowingly made false promises and behaved unprofessionally.**

In another situation, imagine that you have purchased a water purifier for your house and it is not functioning properly. You want to log a call and dial customer care. The call gets connected immediately and then starts the never-ending IVR (Interactive Voice Response) of the company.

Chapter 3 What Customers Get

It starts with, "Please choose options carefully as our IVR options have changed recently." Then it follows the usual selection like "If you are calling for home appliance, press 1, for industrial products, please press 2." Going ahead you press 1 for a new purchase,

It continues, "If you are an existing customer Press 2." Then follows a series of selections and subselections. After performing this great hand exercise of pressing numbers, somehow you find '9' or '8' which allows you to talk to the customer care executive.

However, the journey does not end here and you receive an important automated message saying, "Dear Customer, all our executives are currently busy talking to other customers. Your time is important to us, we will connect you to our executive at the earliest. Estimated wait time is 60 seconds." This is followed by a promotional message or the official music of the company. You still keep your cool and wait for the executive to join.

The executive joins the call and says, "Hello Devendra! Thank you for calling us. How can I help you?." Now, it is again up to you to explain what product you have, what the problem is, when you purchased it, etc. The executive does not find the extended warranty details you are mentioning in the system and says he will connect you to the right department. He politely takes your permission to put you on hold and connects you to the next person who also starts with the same questions the previous gentlemen had asked. You have no option but to give details again. The only non-repetitive detail is your name but that too you may have to confirm by giving your date of birth or your mother's name. In the end, you feel completely exhausted due to the **tiring and ineffective customer complaint logging system the company has deployed.**

Imagine one more situation where you are visiting a mall for shopping. There you meet a person who offers you a lucky draw without any purchase. You just need to share basic information like your name, date of birth, mobile number and occupation. You are requested to fill up a small coupon and a counter receipt is given to you for claiming the prize. You forget about the draw and do not receive any call from the person. But you start getting calls for various products like home loans, personal loans, credit cards and other financial help. Sometimes you apply for a demat account to buy a mutual fund and start getting calls and messages about trading tips. You will feel insecure as few **players are trading your information and data without your knowledge for their benefit.**

Ideally, I should apologize to you all for making you imagine the above situations for yourself. Many of you would have been reminded of bad experiences you had in the past. And by the way, the list only starts with the above situations. There will be many more reasons and instances where the customer feels dissatisfied. I made you go through this, to help you be in the customer's shoes. The more you think from the customer's point of view in your area of work, the better you become. We must avoid any situation for our customers, where we would not like to be if the role reverses.

Why I touched upon the emotions customers feel in these situations is to help all of us to be more **empathetic towards customers**. What is empathy? **It's the ability to understand another person's thoughts and feelings in a situation from their point of view, rather than your own.** Empathy is not sympathy because sympathy is where one is moved by the thoughts and feelings of another but maintains an emotional distance.

Empathy is key when dealing with customer complaints and requests. I will elaborate in further chapters on how one can use empathy in managing a challenging customer situation.

Now the question is, how do we know what customers think or feel about our product/service when we are the provider (seller)? The answer is very simple; ask no one but the customer themselves. Yes! **customer feedback** is the best way. There can be many ways by which customer feedback can be taken—verbal, written, formal, informal, qualitative, quantitative, etc. The method by which customer feedback is to be taken depends upon the respective business context and industry norms.

Out of many ways of capturing customer feedback, I will explain step by step process for formal written feedback which can be adopted with relevant customization.

Step 1: Decide the scope of the feedback survey.

(a) First thing you need to decide is whether the entire end-to-end process should be covered under customer feedback or if you want to focus on only specific aspects of your product/service. The end-to-end process means the customer will give feedback on all the stages of their interaction and experience with you i. e. marketing, communication, design, sales, pricing, usage, and service. Specific aspects will mean that you will go deeper into some of the areas mentioned above. In my opinion, an end-to-end scope should be considered first, and only when the provider is at good satisfaction levels and wants to improve performance further, specific areas should be taken up.

(b) Another part is to decide the sample size. There are many studies and research studies done on sampling techniques. However, based on my experience, my suggestion to people starting this journey will be to try and cover 80% of your customers chosen randomly. However, in case the total customer count is very big, respondents should be capped at a maximum of 1000.

(c) Feedback should cover all the categories/subcategories applicable to your business/profession (as identified under Chapter 2). Analysis of the outcome of feedback should be on this basis for identifying specific actions. Feedback should also be conducted in a manner that allows you to see customer group-based outcomes.

Step 2: Decide on the entity which will conduct the survey.

Customer feedback can be taken directly by the provider or a 3rd party professional agency can be deployed. When a survey is conducted directly it is cost-effective. However, some customers may not be very candid in their feedback. Whereas if the survey is conducted by a 3rd party and the customer is offered the option of hiding their identity, unfiltered feedback is ensured. You can decide which model to adopt. The important point is to start collecting customer feedback. In today's digital world, it is possible to do surveys without any cost.

Step 3: Choosing the feedback scale

It Should be done carefully. The most commonly used scale is a rating between 1 to 10, where 1 is the lowest rating and 10 is the highest. It becomes easy for respondents to attach a number with the same logic to different areas of feedback. However, what a number denotes should be explained to customers in advance so that difference in their understanding does not affect the survey outcome. For example:

Rating	10	9-8	7-6	5	4-3	2-1
Denotes	Excellent	Very Good	Good	Average	Below Average	Poor

You may customize these rating ranges and meanings as per your business.

Similarly, a 5 Point Scale (Likert scale) can be used with or without numeric input if we want to capture respondents' sentiments.

Rating	Strongly Agree	Agree	Neutral	Disagree	Strongly Disagree

You would have observed that many of the shopping stores have started taking feedback on a three-point scale as well. That is to capture user sentiment very quickly and they cover almost 100% of the customers. Colour-coded smileys are used to help customers make quick decisions.

Step 4: Decide the survey format and questions.

(a) The first part of the survey should explain and give context to the customer on why we are doing this survey and how we will use their feedback. This brings customer alignment and interest in the process. The expected time required to fill out the survey should also be stated at the start.

(b) The second part should capture basic details about the customer to identify relevant customer groups. This will help us do segmented analysis which will lead to better actions.

(c) The questionnaire ideally should cover feedback in the form of ratings (quantitative) and open-ended responses (qualitative). The Ratings will help you understand which areas are strongest or weakest. Whereas responses under open-ended questions will give you reasons for the ratings. A good analysis of customer comments will automatically lead you to the root cause of a problem and a probable solution. Examples of both are as below.

Quantitative Q - Please rate our Product for its Quality on a scale of 1 to 10 where 1 is the lowest and 10 is the highest.

Response (Please Tick) - 1 2 3 4 5 6 7 8 9 10

Qualitative Q - Your suggestions on how we can make our service more customer-centric.

Response (open-ended) -

Step 5: Launch the survey.

Based on customer preference, you may choose to do a survey in physical format or through online/digital tools which are already available in the market. A one-on-one interview can be done with senior leaders/professionals. It may require additional time, effort, and money but I am sure that insights from the interviews will be worth the investment.

A survey should be launched with a targeted response count within a pre-decided timeline and extensions should be avoided. The frequency of the next survey will depend on the nature of the business, the scale of the Business, and how much time it generally takes to bring in improvement based on feedback. For example, a partnership firm of law practitioners can bring improvement very fast if all partners agree on a solution. Whereas an MNC will take some time to improve its working which may be driven by global standards as deviations are not accepted easily.

FMCG businesses may want to take feedback every quarter of the year as the competition is very high and customer preferences change faster.

The only thing you need to keep in mind is that the first survey gives you the baseline performance and you must continue the practice of conducting customer feedback surveys to see how the performance is moving over time.

Step 6: Respond to the outcome.

The most critical part of the feedback cycle is to take action based on the survey. You will be able to decide on action steps after understanding the root cause of the problems customers are speaking about. There are many tools and techniques which help us understand the correct root cause. There has to be a sincere effort to address the root cause and change should be visible to customers. The speed of changes matters and hence should be done expeditiously. In fact, our effort should be to reach a level where the customer believes that if they give feedback, the provider will make changes to their product/service. I will be elaborating on this in the next chapter.

It is also important to keep communicating about changes you are bringing due to customer feedback. There are chances that customers might not notice big improvements and thus do not appreciate your approach eventually.

Other Ways of Capturing Customer Feedback

In many businesses taking formal feedback is not possible or not preferred by customers such as when you are dealing with a government organization for providing material or executing a project for them. The officials either may be unreachable or may not be inclined to participate in a formal feedback survey. In such situations, you may capture their indirect feedback. You may see their comments in inspection reports or audit reports or you may simply talk to them and get informal/unofficial comments.

When customers are in very senior positions, an appointment can be taken for a one-on-one interview, where their views and inputs can be captured on your product/service. A few must-ask questions during such interviews are - where they see their organization moving towards in the next 3-5 years or how we can support them in realizing their plans or where we need to improve considering the industry's future. The insights coming from these questions will lead you to be ready for the future.

Sometimes, focus group discussions are also used to capture customer feedback and opinion. Having focus groups is a research method where a group of customers are invited for a group discussion. Each person in the group is encouraged to participate in a discussion that is pre-planned by a researcher and guided by a facilitator. The discussions are analyzed thereafter.

A newer way of capturing customer feedback and sentiments is through social media. Companies regularly monitor what is said about them by users on platforms like Twitter, Facebook, Instagram, Yelp, and a variety of other social media, blogs and review sites. Although these comments should not be used as conclusive results on customer feedback because dissatisfied customers are expected to use these platforms more than satisfied customers.

Capturing customer feedback is important, methods for the same can best be decided by you.

The reader's next task will sum up this chapter.

Task 5: Customer Feedback Survey

Readers will immediately decide on the plan for capturing customer feedback with or without a formal survey. The formal survey is to be designed with help of the steps provided above.

After going through all the chapters of this book, readers must relook at the plan they have prepared and enhance it if required. Once the final plan is in place, execute the same.

Chapter 4

Balancing Want & Get

In earlier chapters, we tried to understand what customers want and what they get. Companies and professionals who understand the gap between what customers want and what they get are best positioned to leverage it. It is like a doctor who first needs to understand the cause of the patient's discomfort before treatment can be started. He must interact with the patient directly and tries to assess the cause. If an interaction is not sufficient, he must ask for diagnostic tests to be sure of the root cause. However, knowing the cause may not help if the doctor does not align his treatment with the cause. Similarly, taking action to align the way of working is essential to leverage this opportunity to win customers. I will talk about some proven and useful approaches to help readers take the right actions.

Long-term Direction

In Chapter 1, I briefly mentioned the role of top leaders in creating a customer-focused mindset for others in the team to follow. If the leader is not convinced that their role has to be that of a provider, which is way above that of a seller, nothing will move. Leaders set the direction for the team by telling the purpose of the organization and what is their vision for their future.

These two terms, purpose and vision are very important not only for the bigger organizations but also for proprietary firms and professionals alike. The only difference is that generally it is not stated in so many words for proprietary firms and individual professionals. The reason is that they subconsciously know why they are doing what they do, and where they want to reach. Still, my recommendation is that all my readers opt for the stated purpose and vision. The benefit of having them stated will be that when in doubt, you can see which of the available choices is aligned with your purpose and vision.

Deciding the purpose and vision for yourself has to be a systematic assisted exercise. Here, I am only giving you the basics about the purpose and vision.

What is Purpose?

The purpose simply can be explained as your reason for existence. Why are you there? The purpose is defined at a higher level and generally is a noble one. The purpose inspires and drives the organization and individuals alike. From the "Win With Your Customer" point of view, it relates very well with the provider's way of thinking.

Some of the customer-centric purposes of organizations from the Fortune 500 companies list are as follows. (Brand 2021)

"We help customers realize their hopes and dreams by providing the best products and services to protect them from life's uncertainties and prepare them for the future."

"To help more and more people experience financial well-being."

"To help our customers achieve their goals by providing them with the technology advice and products they need when they need them."

"We innovate to find a better way for the clients who depend on us, the customers who rely on them, and the communities who count on us all."

"To champion every client's goal with passion and integrity."

"To provide our policyholders with as near perfect protection, as near perfect service as is humanly possible and to do so at the lowest possible cost."

"To advance the way people live and work."

What is a Vision?

A vision is an aspirational destiny that you want to reach or something you want to achieve in line with your purpose. A vision is more action-oriented and allows people to work towards planning and executing supporting strategy. Some examples of vision statements of well-known companies are as below. (Keenan 2022)

Amazon: "To be Earth's most customer-centric company; to build a place where people can come to find and discover anything they might want to buy online."

Disney: "To be one of the world's leading producers and providers of entertainment and information."

Southwest Airlines: "To be the world's most loved, most efficient, and most profitable airline."

Coca-Cola: "To craft the brands and choice of drinks that people love."

Aligning With Others

Having a purpose and vision only on paper will not help. Leaders will have to communicate these with easy-to-understand explanations to their team members and suppliers/partners alike. In fact, at a higher level of maturity, the selection and continuation of suppliers/partners will be driven based on their alignment with your purpose and vision. It is also critical that you define certain quantifiable milestones which will account for vision realization. For example, if your vision is to become the most customer-centric company, you can have milestones such as the following:

(i) Achieve more than 90% 4 Star rating for product XYZ.
(ii) Reduce customer complaints by 50% in the next 3 years.
(iii) Achieve and sustain 70+ NPS in the next 5 years.

Many organizations define a separate mission statement for themselves which helps them realize their vision through a broader but achievable target.

So, now the next task for the readers is to find a purpose and vision for themselves.

Task 6: Setting the direction and aligning with others.

(A) If you already have a stated purpose and vision, please revisit your existing purpose & vision. Evaluate if they clearly indicate your preference to work towards making the customer a winner. If not, take a fresh look and recraft the purpose and vision.

(B) If you do not have a stated purpose and vision, you may have to take the help of a facilitator to conduct a proper workshop to arrive at a customer-focused purpose and vision.

Accordingly, plan and execute communication and alignment actions for the purpose and vision for all the relevant stakeholders.

Value Creation Focus

To become a provider (from a seller) for the customer, we need to design (or relook) our product and services with a perspective of value. We need to evaluate in what sense we are adding value to a customer's life. Whatever we do through our products and services has to benefit customers in some way or the other.

To understand this better, let's ask ourselves a simple question. Why does the customer want any product/service? Because in front of them, they have some task/job which they need to do. To finish this task/job they want to use suitable products/services. This is one level deeper than the customer's need we understood earlier. To fulfill their own need, customers are supposed to do certain jobs for which they may seek products/services. **For example,** travelling from one place to another is a customer need. To fulfill this need, customers are supposed to do tasks/jobs like booking tickets, accommodation, local travel booking, carrying baggage, etc.

Now, the customers cannot or maybe do not want to do all these jobs themselves. That's why they will look for some product/service which can do these jobs for them in the manner they expect. That is how services like Make My Trip (an online portal showing all the options for travel in one place with an easy-to-use interface—does customers' job of searching and booking various airlines in few clicks), Air BNB (for verified stay arrangements), Uber (for local travel with information on ETA, cost, route, etc.), etc. will be preferred. While carrying baggage at the airport products like baggage trolly, escalators, elevators, etc. will be used.

Now, think about why customers do not want to do these jobs. They do not want to do so because either it is difficult (painful) to do or someone else can do the job better than them (gainful). These two reasons are very important to understand while designing your product/service. The customer will look for a Product/ Service only if it is either **a pain reliever or gain creator.**

For example, a customer takes a taxi for local travel as it reduces the pain of someone dropping them off (in terms of time-saving and inconvenience reduction). Whereas the customer will prefer Uber over local taxis as it creates gain for them (in terms of convenience of booking, ease of payment, safer trackable ride, etc.). The product/service that we want customers to use must be designed to either relieve pain or create a gain for them. Pain and gain can be in areas of time, money, effort, experience, feelings, quality, performance, obstacles, social standing, etc. **Simply put, pain relief is like reducing the negatives from a customer's life and creating gain is like enhancing the positives.**

When a product/service is designed for the above, it is bound to be accepted and appreciated by the customers. In today's era, with technological enhancements, fantastic innovations are being done by companies. Companies are continuously looking for opportunities where they can address customers' pain and gain. Not only are new products/ services being launched, but improvements in existing ones are also being done.

Now, let's understand how to go about identifying customers' pain and gain. To do this, we need to go through the journey that the customers take and look for opportunities for relieving pain or creating gain. We need to first select a need customers want to fulfill. Then, we see what jobs (actions) customers have to do to fulfill this need. As a trial case, this can be done assuming we are the customers. However, to do this more scientific user research (through interviews, observation, focus group studies, surveys, etc.) is needed. For now, let's do a simple exercise where we will select one customer need and try to

Chapter 4 Balancing Want & Get

understand related tasks/jobs and the associated pain and gain. The simplified flow to do this is as below -

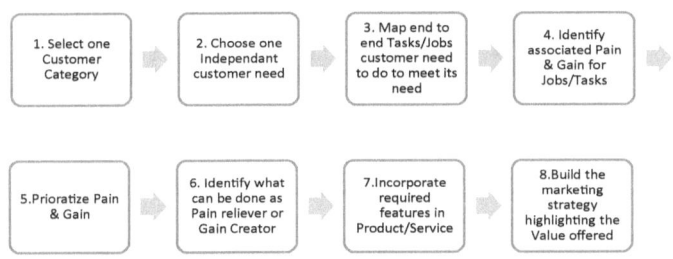

Illustration -

1. We take the customer category as a senior citizen couple living in an urban area. Their children are working abroad.
2. Let's take the couple's basic need of consuming appropriate food.
3. & 4. Illustrative table as below:

Tasks/Jobs	Associated Pain/Gain
• Purchase of grocery	• Need to go to a crowded market. • Need to go to the vegetable market, then to the grocery shop, then to the dairy. • Have to carry the bags from the gate to the elevator • Difficult to manage in the rainy season. • Will be great if they don't need to handle cash for the purchase.

Continued...

• Cooking/ Ordering Food	• Don't want to cook all the time. • Can't eat outside food as routine. • Hotels do not provide food with less salt/sugar levels. • Kitchen helper takes a lot of leave at the last moment. • Will be great if they don't need to worry about balancing their diet as per the doctor's advice.

Now observe this. How many business models have already been identified and launched considering the above pain and gain in the last couple of decades? For example:

- Big retail supermarkets provide a one-stop solution where groceries, fresh vegetables, fruits, etc. can be purchased at the same time.
- They started a home delivery service for groceries if the bill is above a minimum purchase value.
- E-Commerce services like Big Basket and Amazon Fresh deliver the grocery to your doorstep.
- Models like self-pickup points have been launched by D Mart.
- 10-15 mins delivery models like Zepto and Dunzo.
- Diet meal plans with customization options and goal-based advice by Fitmeals, Activate, Eatfit, etc.
- Routine or occasional cooks through Cookzy, thechefcart (available in limited cities as of now).

We are in a world where we hear new startups being launched every other day trying to specialize in a niche and solve the smallest of problems for consumers. In this scenario, if we do not acquire a high focus on customer value enhancement, we are going to lose. This brings us to a very important task for readers to complete next.

Task 7: Identify value enhancement for customers.

Sequentially, take each of the primary customer categories identified under tasks 2 and 3. For each of the primary categories of customers, you must follow steps 1 to 6 as per the flow and illustration that has been given above.

The outcome of this task will be ideas for improvement or a new offering. After evaluating ideas and taking into consideration the efforts versus impact or cost versus benefits, you must take this ahead.

Use of Identified Expectations

After reading the last paragraph, you must be wondering what the difference between customer pain and gain is as opposed to expectations. Since both are correlated with customer needs directly and we have identified them under different tasks, let me clarify. We saw that customer expectation is **how a customer wants to meet their need**. If we try and understand the reason behind 'how,' we will find customer pain & gain. All the known customer pains and gains can be easily seen by the customers themselves. If customers can see the pain and gain in the process, they start addressing this pain and gain themselves. They think about the solutions and start converting them into articulated expectations.

The realization of pain and gain also comes from experience. **For example**, for a small get-together, a couple orders 25 pizzas. The order comes on time but is delivered by one person. While handling the pile of pizzas, one of the boxes gets damaged even though the pizza inside was intact. It was a bit awkward for the couple to give a damaged box to their guest. The customer understood the pain in the process and identified the solution; one person must not carry a large number of pizzas together. So, the next time when they ordered pizzas for a party, they gave instructions that two delivery people should bring their order in half quantity each to make sure the boxes are not damaged. They even did further checking at the time of delivery to ensure proper handling.

The takeaway for every provider (seller) is that they must understand that many times customer expectations seem unreasonable. However, that may be due to the customer's experience or a situation of which we are not aware. That is why an empathetic approach is needed at each stage of customer handling.

Any professional or organization will benefit immensely if they can identify customer pain and gain which are not obvious and not visible to customers themselves **(as done under Task 7)**. When we identify what we can do to address these hidden pains and gains, we are addressing the unarticulated (Unsaid) expectation of customers. A combination of meeting both articulated and unarticulated expectations creates a delightful customer experience, which we are aiming to provide ultimately.

Let me give **an example of an unarticulated need** being addressed which creates a better customer experience. In many cars, you will find a feature of a kick sensor. That means there is no need to manually open the boot and with a small foot movement, the boot will open automatically. Now, do you think many customers would have articulated the pain which they had to go through while handling the luggage? They had to either put luggage on the floor or the car roof or take someone's help. One of the auto companies saw this process and identified this pain. That is how an innovative solution of kick sensors was introduced. Customers will be delighted and willing to pay an additional price as this feature addresses their unarticulated needs. Proof of this theory is that this feature generally comes in the higher variant of cars that are in the premium segment. It is a different fact that today's newness (Novelty) will be tomorrow's usual. That is why, I say, that this journey is a continuous one.

If you are following this path, you will be successful and always stay ahead of your competition. I will elaborate on how we can be ahead of our competition in a subsequent chapter.

Use of Customer Feedback

Under Chapter 3, I have explained the importance of collecting customer feedback and the key steps to be followed for launching a formal customer feedback survey. I assume that you have already conducted your first formal customer feedback as per Task 5. Now, I want to talk about what to do with the outcome of customer feedback.

a) Mindset and Approach

The first important thing is to start by reminding ourselves about the two golden rules I talked about at the start of this book. Accordingly, before reading the outcome of the feedback, remember the purpose of this exercise, which is to know what customers want, how they feel about our product/service, what things they like the most, and what they do not like. Their feedback is for our improvement and not against individuals.

b) Whole to Part

While trying to understand the feedback, we should go from a whole to a part. This means that first we should see the feedback at the overall level and identify improvement points. After that, further segmentation as per the available data and the nature of the business should be done. Ideally, one by one we should go from the overall level to LoB/product level to a broader category level to a subcategory level to customer groups to the individual customer. Appropriate tools/methods for finding the root cause where customer ratings are lower should be used, for example, 5 Why, Pareto, Fishbone, Scatter Diagram, etc. With the identification of the right root cause, improvement actions can suitably be implemented.

It Is also important to go through and understand the open-ended comments given by customers as generally, these comments hint at the pain/gain customers face in the process.

c) Low-Hanging Fruits

After the identification of improvement areas is done, quick actions are expected. To gain momentum, you should identify the actions which are easy to implement with minimum resistance or difficulty level. These actions must be taken without any delay and due to their very nature, they are called low-hanging fruits. In the process of creating a perfect solution, we must not lose the opportunity to take action on these low-hanging fruits.

d) Prioritization and Roadmap

Taking action on all the points at the same time is not possible, in a majority of cases. Thus, prioritization will be needed. Many organizations fail in this because they do not do systematic prioritization and generally actions are taken as per the intuition or judgment of one or two people. One of the ways to go systematically is to first create a basic 2X2 prioritization matrix for the broader areas of improvement. There can be different parameters that can be used to create a 2X2 matrix. However, one easy way will be to have scales such as the effort required to improve versus the value it has for customers. The improvement areas will be rated high or low on both scales. Prioritization will be done as per the position of the improvement area in the respective quadrant. The possible outcome will be as follows.

(i) Low effort, high value—do now
(ii) High effort, high value—do next
(iii) Low effort, low value—do later
(iv) High effort, low value—don't do

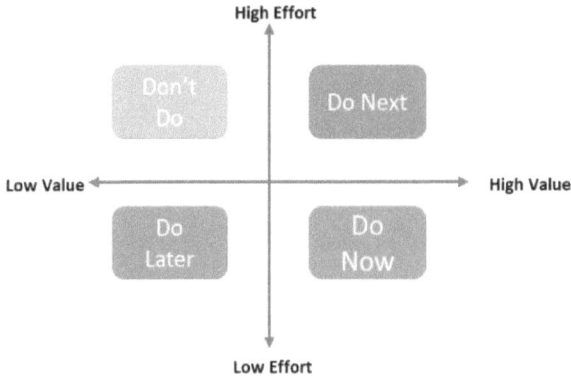

e) Implement and Communicate

Obviously, the next stage is the implementation of ideas. Communicating back to customers while saying that we are thankful for the feedback and have initiated actions based on their feedback is very important. The more they see actions based on their voice, the more they will take the survey seriously. Companies/individuals taking actions based on users' voices are bound to have a better impression of their brand in customers' minds.

f) Trend Analysis

To verify if we are improving or not, a trend of the outcome can be created and used. One-time feedback survey outcome can only give current/spot results. Whereas, when the results are compared with the previous instances, they tell a story. We can also judge where we are headed. We need to look for patterns and insights from the survey trends.

g) Continuous Target improvement

To have a quantifiable challenge, you must set a target for the next cycle of the feedback survey. For example, if the average customer rating for the quality of service is 6 on a scale of 10 in 2023, you should target a rating of 8 in 2024. Obviously, the rating will not improve only by wishing for it. We need to identify actions that will actually improve the quality of service which customers will appreciate in the form of a better rating. A proven technique for improving performance is called benchmarking. Here, you try to learn from people who are better than you. I will elaborate on the benchmarking approach in subsequent chapters.

h) Sustain Strength & Improve Weakness

Many times, this factor is forgotten by the people acting on customer feedback. Just as you must work on weaker areas, similar attention is needed to sustain stronger areas. For example, assume you are in the business of servicing air conditioners. Your customer rating in quality is 9 whereas timeliness is 7. When you identify the root cause you find that service is getting delayed because the number of technicians is not sufficient. Immediately, you recruit 5 additional technicians and start sending them to attend to the complaints. As a result, timeliness is improved, however, the same complaints are surfacing again. This has happened because the new technicians are sent without adequate training. While giving more focus on the weakness, an existing strength was compromised in this case. This type of solution is not good in the long run and thus, should be avoided.

Now that we have learnt a lot about what to do with customer feedback, let's do an evaluative Task.

Task 8: Revalidate your process of customer feedback.

The task is to evaluate and improve your post-feedback approaches. Please use points given under a) to h) and do the same for yourself.

Use of Customer Complaints

The next important approach is the use of customer complaints to identify customers' pain and gain and the opportunities where we can improve ourselves. The core steps for using the complaints are similar to the use of customer feedback.

The only difference is that rather than the customer giving you ratings on your performance, here the customer tells you problems they are facing directly. Attitude, root cause identification, taking action, customer communication, data analysis, trend and pattern identification, analysis of comments, etc. remain the same.

That way customer complaints become a reliable source of data and information for improvement. To show an actual application, I am sharing the way complaint analysis is done by the winners of the CII-EXIM Award for Business Excellence, years 2021 and 2022–Godrej Construction (Business Division of Godrej & Boyce Mfg. Co. Ltd. - https://www.godrej.com/godrej-construction).

Godrej Construction captures customer data systematically. Availability of data ensures correct analysis and root cause analysis. For capturing the data, IT-enabled tools and systems are used. Each complaint is assigned a unique number and the key details captured are mentioned in the table below. The below data is from their Construction Engineering Services department who manages and maintains residential apartments given to company employees for the duration of their employment.

Complaint details are captured under the following headings:

Complainant Number	Flat Number	Complaint Status
Complaint Description	Urgency of complaint	Complaint Resolution Date

Continued...

Chapter 4 Balancing Want & Get

Type Of Customer (Segment-based)	Complaint Date	Targeted SLA
Location Of Customer	Complaint Category	Actual SLA met
Complaint Mode/ Medium	Complaint Type	Amount Chargeable to Customer
Building Type	Department Responsible	Amount Chargeable to Company
Building Number	Contractor Assigned	Remark

You must be wondering what the use of capturing so many details about complaints is. Godrej Construction does a lot of trend and root cause analysis based on the above details. I will show you in a sequence how that is done. Let me take one important aspect of customer complaint - SLA (Service Level Agreement) as an example. SLA is a promise or assurance to customers on the maximum time needed to address their complaints. For example, when you log a complaint for any appliance, generally the company tells you that your complaint will be attended to by a technician within 24 hours. This commitment of 24 hrs is the SLA between you and the company. Different types of complaints may have different SLAs.

So, coming back to SLA data and analysis. I will use the same graphs and methods that Godrej Construction uses, however, the data given in the graphs will not be actual data.

First, the team will look at the overall performance trend on meeting SLAs -

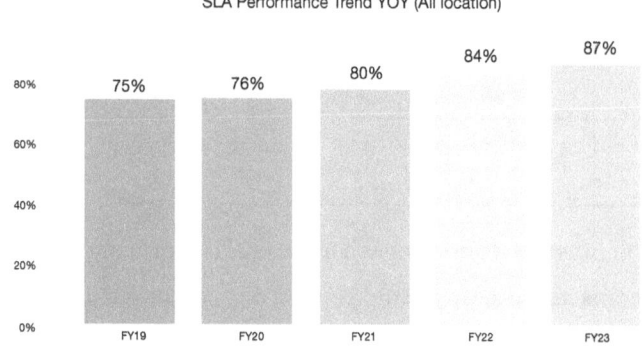

SLA Performance Trend YOY (All location)

We can see from the graph that they have data for the last 5 years which helps them see their progress. The percentage of complaints resolved within the set SLA is improving but is still at a level of 87%. As a customer focussed company, they would want to improve it further. Thus. they will look at the recent performance by bifurcating it into different locations.

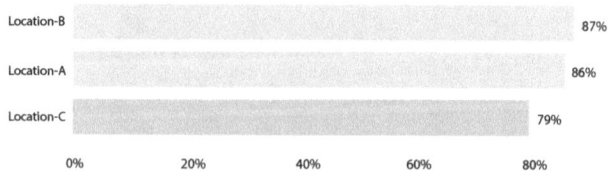

Location Wise SLA Performance (Current FY)

Chapter 4 Balancing Want & Get

Looking at the data, one can easily see that complaints coming from Location C are last in terms of meeting the set SLA. Thus, further analysis is required for Location C.

Category Wise SLA Breakup (Location C)

Category	SLA Performance
Plumbing	85.9%
Drainage	90.0%
Glazing	81.3%
Masonry	64.4%
Fitter	61.3%
Carpentry	69.1%
Welding	54.1%
Others	55.6%
Miscellaneous	100.0%
Painting	100.0%

Number of Complaints

When complaints are seen based on a broad category, the following insights are emerging.

Complaints in the category of plumbing and drainage are getting resolved in time despite high numbers (500+), whereas categories such as masonry, fitter, carpentry and welding are not performing despite their count being low. The team would now go into further detail in each of the lower-performing categories. One example of carpentry is as below.

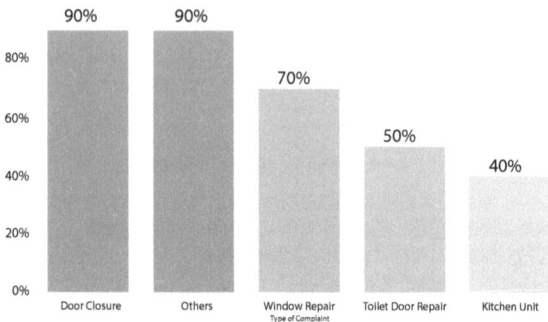

The graph indicates that under carpentry complaints, the kitchen unit and toilet door repair are the areas of great concern. On analyzing the toilet door repair complaints, the team finds that in many cases doors are required to be ordered as they need replacement and the purchase of new doors takes time. That is why SLAs are breached. Now, based on this analysis, the following actions can be initiated:

(a) A quality revalidation will be done to see if the doors in use are adequately suitable. Appropriate alternatives will be identified.

(b) In case the alternative is chosen, whenever replacement is needed, a new variety of doors will be used.

(c) The comparative performance of alternative doors will be monitored.

(d) Attic stock (a few doors as a standby in stock) will be maintained for doors so that the wait for the purchase of new doors is eliminated and customer complaints are resolved immediately.

The team will look at the kitchen unit complaints as well. Here, the model is through outsourcing and this is because kitchen units are provided by another company and only authorized technicians are supposed to attend to the complaints. Under this model, multiple registered vendors (contractors) are enrolled and based on workload and technician availability they attend to the complaints. Thus, data will be seen from a contractor performance point of view -

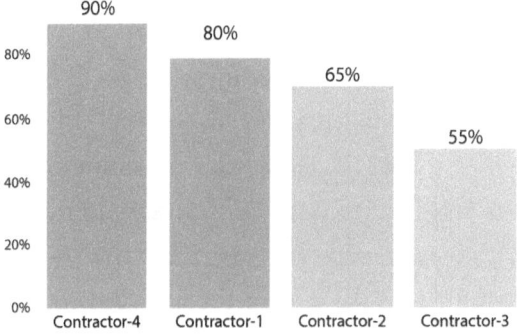

Contractor Wise SLA Breakup (Carpenter)

The data suggests low performance by contractors 2 & 3. Now, the company has the option to go to these contractors and ask why their performance is not on par with others. There can be further root cause analysis to understand what challenges are faced by these contractors.

Reason for Contractor's Performance

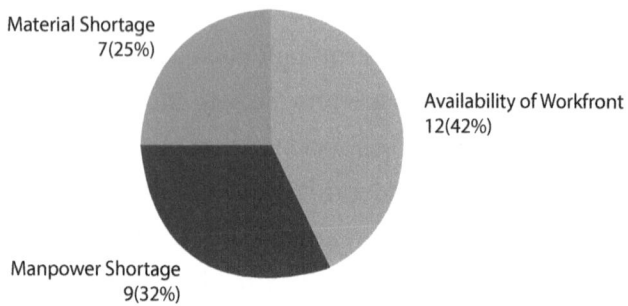

The outcome of further analysis suggests that 42% of the time, the work front is not available for work, whereas the balance is due to a shortage of manpower/material. In this scenario, the following actions will be taken:

(a) Communication for confirming availability with customers will be enhanced.

(b) In case there is a delay from the customer side, the 'On Hold' status will be introduced and informed to the customer. This on hold time will not be attributed to the contractor and shall be deducted from the SLA calculation.

(c) The manufacturing company of the kitchen unit will be persuaded to improve their delivery time for providing material to contractors.

(d) The contractors will be persuaded to increase the number of trained technicians for faster response.

Chapter 4 Balancing Want & Get

Hopefully, you would have got some idea of how customer complaints and analysis can be used for identifying required action. The available data can be seen from more angles and different insights can be identified. The above analysis on meeting customer SLA is only one example from Godrej Construction.

The important thing to remember is that customer service plays a key role in building your brand value. It is the service that differentiates you from others in the market. The transactional relationship becomes a collaborative relationship with customers through good service. In fact, service has become a new business model like Annual Maintenance Contract (AMC) provided by Original Equipment Manufacturers (OEM). Thus, this area must not be ignored.

To summarize, under Chapter 4 of 'Balancing Want & Get' we saw the following key approaches:
- **Long term Direction**
- **Aligning Others**
- **Value Creation Focus**
- **Pain Relieving & Gain Creation**
- **Use of Identified Expectations**
- **Use of Customer Feedback**
- **Use of Customer Complaints**

Now that we have learnt a lot about the customers, it's time to check what we have learnt. Thus, I have created a small quiz for the readers. Please attempt the quiz on your own. Correct answers are at the end of the book.

Q1: Complete the Sentence - "If the customer is ever wrong, _____"

Q2: Choose the right answer.

When we categorize customers as kids, adults and senior citizens, what is the basis of categorization?

(a) Demography-Based (b) Geography-Based

(c) Association-Based (d) Product/Service-Based

Q3: Does the given statement relate to customer needs or expectations?

"I just woke up; I need a cup of tea"

(a) Need (b) Expectation

Q4: Does the given statement relate to customer needs or expectations? "The tea is not warm enough. Bring it in a neat and clean cup"

(a) Need (b) Expectation

Chapter 4 Balancing Want & Get

Q5: Is the statement true or false?

The best way to understand customers' problems is to be sympathetic toward them.

(a) True (b) False

Q6: Is the statement true or false?

One can get customer feedback by having a discussion with them.

(a) True (b) False

Q7: Which of the following are core for setting a long-term direction?

(a) Customer Needs (b) Customer Experience

(c) Purpose (d) Vision

Q8: Tag the following actions/scenarios as either customers' pain relievers or gain creators.

(i) My local grocery shop has recently started home delivery if the order is more than Rs. 200. ------- Pain Reliever/Gain Creator

(ii) My milkman has recently started home delivery of curd and buttermilk as well. ------- Pain Reliever/Gain Creator

(iii) The government of India has also started an online service to apply for a passport. ------- Pain Reliever/ Gain Creator

(iv) We get status updates via SMS and Email whenever the passport-making process goes to the next stage. ------- Pain Reliever / Gain Creator

(v) The municipal authority has made the tender process completely digital for the contractors. ------- Pain Reliever/Gain Creator

Q9: Match the columns based on the prioritization matrix explained for actions as a result of customer feedback.

Actionable Characteristic	Prioritization
Low Effort, High Value	Do Later
High Effort, High Value	Do Next
Low Effort, Low Value	Don't Do
High Effort, Low Value	Do Now

Chapter 5

How Much to Communicate

Can anyone deny that without communication the universe cannot work? Human beings cannot function without communication and I am sure each one of us is dealing with customers who are human only. Even if you're an NGO working for animal welfare, where the end users are animals, you need to communicate with them. Body language, touch and warmth may take the place of spoken language, but communication will be needed. Otherwise, how would you explain a stray dog allowing few people to play with her newborn puppies while she is aggressive with others?

Each one of us knows that to maintain any relationship, a required level of communication needs to be understood well. If the communication need is met, the relationship remains stronger and can withstand rough times. When we say we want to win with the customer, basically it is creating a relationship where we are putting all our efforts into making the customers win. When a customer wins, they understand the value we are offering and start considering us as their partner. The relationship then develops into a long-term association if not active collaboration.

When to Communicate

If someone asks me this question, my simple answer will be **always."** Yes! You must always communicate with your customers. However, 'what,' 'how,' and 'how much' will change as per customer need and stage of the customer journey. For example, you need not communicate your terms of post-warranty service in the marketing promotion. If you are sending an SMS status of delivery for an item purchased, you need not mention the price at which it was purchased. To decide the what, how and how much, let us map the stages the customers go through. The stages will be almost similar for all customers although details may differ. The customers' journey is generally divided into 5 stages:

1. **Awareness:** In this stage, customers become familiar with the brand through advertising, word-of-mouth, or social media. They see the brands around them and capture what the brand/company/professional is offering and what they stand for.
2. **Consideration:** In this stage, based on their needs and expectations, customers actively consider whether to

buy or not the product or service which is offered. They compare available options for making an informed decision.

3. **Purchase** - Here, customers do the actual purchase. This is a stage where creating customer experience becomes highly important. Customer-centric communication plans will help a seamless transition in this stage.

4. **Retention:** In this stage, customers use the product and seek support and guidance from the provider. They get contacted by the provider to encourage brand loyalty. The level of post-sale service determines customer delight which makes customers your promoter or detractor.

5. **Advocacy:** Here, the customer spreads the word about the product, service, or experience. It may be positive or negative. Through this book, we are trying to make customers our brand ambassadors and promoters. If messaging and actual delivery does not match across the previous 4 stages, there is no chance that customers will advocate for us.

Thus, we need to take into account customers' communication needs and expectations at each of the stages and various customer touch points under each stage.

Customer touchpoints are your brand's points of customer contact during different stages of the customer journey. For example, customers may find out about your service online or through an advertisement, see ratings and reviews, visit your website, shop at your retail store, or contact your customer service. All these are customer touch points. In short, whenever a potential customer or customer comes in contact with your brand, that is a customer touchpoint. Let us now try and systematize communication plans as per customer journey stages.

Illustration:

Stage	Questions that need to be answered (Communication Need)	Few possible communication mediums which can be adopted
Awareness	• What value is offered? • Is a solution available for my problem? • Do I know this Brand? • What does the brand stand for?	Traditional mediums of advertisement, social media, SMS, word of mouth, purpose and vision-based campaigns, brand ambassadors, etc.

Continued...

Chapter 5 How Much to Communicate

Consideration	• What Options are there • Which option is better and how • Technical and commercial comparison • What do my friends say about it? • What is my family's opinion? • What is the customer rating and feedback? • Is an online alternative available on better terms	Social media, word of mouth, 3rd party websites, sales personnel by meeting or tele calling, own website, technical presentations, pamphlets, print & digital media, physical and digital stores, agents, etc.
Purchase	• What is the best way to purchase? • Payment options and Terms • How fast can delivery happen? • What add-on can I get? • Will service be good enough?	Sales executive, terms of purchase and service through an invoice, live tracking option, status update via SMS, app, call, etc. Flexibility of delivery slot selection via website/App etc.

Continued...

Retention	- How to use the product/service? - Where to contact for problem resolution? - When and how will the complaint be resolved? - Will I get charged for the service?	Installation and demonstration, user manual, do's and don'ts, social media videos, customer care, email, proactive service, user feedback, technician visits, etc.
Advocacy/ Loyalty	- Is the quality of the product/service still maintained? - Is there any loyalty benefit available? - What has changed from last time?	Personalized communications and seasonal greetings, repeat/referral policy, birthday offers, get-together, invite to new launches, thank You/appreciation note, etc.

The importance of better communication with customers at all stages of their journey has been understood very well by organizations, especially B2C e-commerce companies. You take any of the companies like Amazon, Flipkart, Zomato, Dunzo, Swiggy, etc. If you observe carefully, through their advertisements on the web, TV, etc., they communicate and sell the value they offer to customers.

Chapter 5 How Much to Communicate

Had this not been the case, how would a customer know that fruits and groceries can be delivered in 15 mins? Amazon addressed the need for a 'No Questions Asked' return policy which made people overcome their hesitancy in ordering online for many things. Returns and cashback are initiated automatically and notifications are sent. Live location of delivery through food delivery apps is now a normal practice and expectation. Estimated time of arrival (ETA) is a must-have and prominent feature. Technology advancement and the adoption of smartphones have accelerated the above enhancements which are proving to be a great experience for customers.

It is not that only new-age businesses are ensuring better customer communication. Even well-established organizations are transforming themselves. Take the example of Indian Post services. There was a time when it was difficult to know when the post or letter would reach its destination except for the telegram services. There were many stories where the posts were either delivered very late or never reached their destination. However, with time, Indian Post realized its customers' needs. And that is how higher-priced services like registered post and speed post were introduced. The registered post ensured acknowledgment from the recipient whereas the speed post offered faster delivery.

On the communication part, speed post initially offered basic need-based reactive tracking of the consignment. A person could either go to the post office or could check on the website. Still, customer communication expectations were not completely met. Learning from the private sector competitors, Indian Post improved a lot on communication. Today, when you book a speed post, you get an SMS immediately. The status of the consignment movement is shared with the recipient via SMS. The name of the postman along with the expected delivery day is also shared.

The reason for giving this example is to show that if a government organization can bring about customer-centric changes, any organization can do it.

Each organization or professional needs to decide the medium/mode of communication as per their understanding of customers. They may choose what, according to them, is the most effective medium. However, they should ensure that the communication addresses the questions to be answered as mentioned in the illustrative table. There are certain principles one can follow for value-adding communication.

Consistent Messaging Across Mediums

In the previous table I illustrated that customer questions that need to be answered change as per the stage of the customer journey. However, as a provider (seller) we need to see what we should be communicating across stages at the beginning itself. Our policies and the way we will respond to customers should be deliberated in advance. People coming in touch with customers should be confident and aware of these responses. Standard protocol and its communication to all the people (including new joiners) is necessary.

For example, assume that you are a law firm and many senior and junior lawyers work with you. You want your firm to be very professional and customer-centric. That is why you have set a few protocols such as the use of an appointment system, limiting waiting time for the client to not be more than 15 mins, proactive communication on case status, explanation of matters in an easy-to-understand manner, and validation of documents before submission. You and your associates have been following these for many years and now a senior advocate is joining your team who is known for making clients wait for long durations. In this case, you need to explain to him the protocols and practices you have established at the time of the interview itself. Thereafter, you may have to reinforce these practices with vigilant observation.

Another example is to have a written service and warranty policy which all the sales people must know about. The same policy should be explained to customers proactively and shared via websites, invoices, warranty manuals, customer care personnel, etc.

Another important consistency messaging is about what you believe in and stand for. It is demonstrating and living for your purpose and vision. For example, your purpose and vision are to provide affordable homes for everyone. Here, you cannot provide a tap or electric fitting which is not easily available in the local market and is imported from other countries. Because, post-warranty, if someone wants to replace the fitting, they should be able to do it with ease and at an affordable price. Your actions should demonstrate your intent across the customer journey and not conflict with itself at any instance.

Updated In-Sync Communication

We know that customer communication today has progressed from a linear single channel to multichannel and now, to omnichannel. The focus is on the customer and not the channel of communication. All communication channels talk the same language and create a unified customer experience. The format has become more conversational-based rather than based on formal language etiquette.

Many people adopt new and improved modes and ways of communication at the start but fail to keep them updated. A common example of this is obsolete contact numbers/ Email IDs/ service centres on websites. Another recent one is the display of Covid-19 protocols without following them as they are no more applicable. This may be due to a lack of interest or the cost of maintenance. In any case, we should put a system in place which updates customer communication with agility.

Listening to Customers

Listening is as important as speaking in the process of communication. Customer communication is no different. One of the core purposes of having a robust communication plan is to get the customer's voice. Not every customer wants to share until there is some issue faced by them. Thus, having an opportunity to get the customer's voice, when there is no complaint, is a luxury. Obviously, formal customer feedback is a great source of the customer's voice. However, informal discussions give you probable areas of gain that today, customers are not even expecting. You need to be alert and pick up those signs. This can be achieved in two ways:

(i) Schedule a routine proactive customer meeting and capture the mood and what is happening around the customer.

(ii) Sensitize people on the ground who come in touch with customers and capture their observations/ inputs for further analysis.

Let me give you an actual example of how it is done by the winners of the CII-EXIM Award for Business Excellence years 2021 and 2022 – Godrej Construction (Business Division of Godrej & Boyce Mfg. Co. Ltd.). The example is from one of their lines of business–Real Estate Leasing. This LoB offers A-Grade office premises to IT companies. Their business is B2B and many international IT companies are their customers. This company is an early adopter of 3rd party customer feedback surveys (since 2010) which is not common industry practice in India. Despite conducting a formal feedback survey, this LoB has put in place a process where the customer engagement calendar is prepared at the start of the year. This engagement calendar allows them to have multilevel interactions and inputs. They track the actual engagement against the plan and capture articulated and unarticulated needs and expectations of clients. Improvements are done accordingly. A portion of this customer engagement calendar is as below:

Team / Person from Godrej Construction	Client Coverage	Team/Person from Client	Frequency
Customer Relationship Managers (CRM)	All Clients	Administration Head	Monthly
Line of Business (LoB) Head	Key Clients	Administration Head/Real Estate Head	Quarterly
Business Head (Godrej Construction)	Key Clients	CEO / COO	Annual
Facility Manager (Appointed by Godrej Construction)	All Clients	Operations Manager	Quarterly

Handling Customer Complaints or Requests

From a customer's perspective, this is the most important stage in terms of communication required from the provider's side because a customer complains when there is some disruption in the job customer is supposed to get done. This creates discomfort, and when someone is in discomfort, they are bound to ask for immediate relief. If the solution is taking time, at least information on when the solution will be achieved is sought. Our communication plan must be prepared to **address the following questions from customers:**

Whom do I call? Are you listening to me? Do you understand my problem? Will you resolve the issue? When will you resolve the issue? Will it be chargeable to me? What is the status? Will it repeat? Why did this happen? How to avoid this in the future?

We should consider the following pointers while designing the plan.

(i) Provide multiple options for logging a call.
(ii) Make complaint logging an easy job.
(iii) Auto SMS/Email based quick acknowledgment system
(iv) Customer complaint and transaction history data to be available with people talking to the customer to avoid repeated questions.
(v) Have a predefined Service Level Agreement (SLA) i.e., how much time it will take to attend to a particular type of complaint. This should be explained to the customer and must not be breached.
(vi) Provide proactive status updates (frequency can be as per the nature of the product/service and its use).
(vii) Provide an escalation matrix so that the customer knows where to go in case of non-resolution. This

may avoid undue use of social media which can damage the brand.

(viii) Trained and ethical service personnel need to be employed.

(ix) Post-complaint resolution and immediate feedback on the solution provided must be taken with an open-ended comment section.

(x) Make a follow-up call to know the effectiveness of the solution and customer experience during the process.

(xi) Use technology-based interventions so that service cost for you is reduced.

Invest in Customer-Focused Skills

Whatever system the owner and top management deploy for customer communication, it is the people down the line who make it successful. The technology can support customer communication to a certain level only. Beyond that responsibility falls to the person who finally meets/speaks to the customer. Customer experience starts when they decide to enter an office/shop. The first person they meet is the security guard at the entry gate. If the guard behaves rudely or unprofessionally, the first impression will be spoiled. Whereas the customer feels happy and welcomed if the guard at entry is humble and polite. No one minds the guard doing his duty if they are well-behaved.

Similarly, all the people coming in contact with customers during the 5 stages of the customer journey create an impression about the organization they represent. Thus, it is very important to invest in training all these people. The degree and type of training and skills required will be different for different people. A simple exercise can help you understand what type of training is to be imparted to the team.

Step 1: Map the customer journey for your product/service considering the 5 stages.

Step 2: Map all the customer touch points where any team member comes in contact with the customer directly.

Step 3: Create a table where unique roles/functions of team members across all the customer touch points are listed.

Step 4: Based on the unique role/function write down the required skills in the next column.

Step 5: Take the help of professional trainers to create programs to enhance the skills identified and send people for the same.

The table will look like this:

Unique Role	Skill Required	Training Needed
Customer Relationship Manager	Communication, empathy, values, writing skills, logical reasoning, escalation management	Purpose-vision-values training, interaction with senior management, conflict management, etc.
Service Technician	Technically sound, listening, speaking, well-groomed	Personal hygiene and grooming, classroom/video/on-the-job training, safety & quality consciousness, etc.
This table can also be used to map all the skills required by team members and a comprehensive training program can be run based on this analysis. I am showing samples only for customer-related skills. Readers should identify unique roles and skills based on the steps explained above.		

To implement what we learned from Chapter 5, let us continue to do the reader's tasks:

Task 9: Transform your customer communication plan as per learnings from Chapter 5.

(a) Map your customer journey under the 5 Stages (awareness, consideration, decision, retention, advocacy).

(b) Identify all possible touch points under the 5 stages and relook at the medium of communication.

(c) Use the principles explained—consistent messaging, updated in-sync communication, and listening to customers.

Task 10: Revalidate the customer complaint-handling process.

Use the pointers given under (i) to (x) and improve.

Task 11: Identify the training needs of the team.

Complete the mapping as per the sample shown and identify the required training modules for all.

Chapter 6

Keeping Them Interested

"Interesting! Let's continue reading. Let's see what else is written in the next chapter, especially the one where I can be ahead of my competition."

Do these lines seem familiar to you? Maybe? I am sure a few of the readers will relate to these lines easily. Similar thoughts would have come to them after reading the initial chapters of this book. If not highly interested each one of you would have been at least mildly interested in this book, right? That is the reason you are continuing to read and I am delighted about this. Even when you decided to purchase this book, you would have gone through the editorial, index, or reviews and found something interesting. Someone would have found the examples interesting and some would have the tasks given under each chapter.

I assume and more importantly, I would love to believe that readers liked this book very much and it has become a bestseller worldwide. I have become famous and well-known because of the success of the book.

Now, I decide to write another book which is on a topic called "Win With Your Employees." I start promoting the book and doing good marketing. Will you purchase it? If your answer is yes, then think about the reason for your decision. I think you will purchase it because, when you see the topic "Win With Your Employees" after reading the first book, you will find it interesting. You may be interested because you want to do something about your employees or you may be interested because you have a few guesses on what topics I might cover in the next book, and you want to confirm if your guesses are right by reading it or you simply like the examples I give.

The lesson learned from this is that customers should find something interesting about your product/service to push them to give it a try initially. While consuming, if the product/service is useful but not interesting enough customers will use it until they find a more interesting or beneficial alternative. As soon as an alternative is viable, they will leave your offering and move on. For example, if you are finding this book useful but not interesting enough to read, you will look if something else is available. Suppose in Google Play Store you find an App (Application) that gives key learnings of this book in audio format, you may be tempted to take it rather than the physical book. Alternatively, if you find that I am doing a free online seminar or a reading session on this book online, you are more likely to join it rather than read the book.

When it comes to customer retention or repeat business, the factor of interest plays a big role. Your willingness to purchase my new book and continue business with me is one such example. When you like my second book as well, you will surely give me a good feedback rating and word-of-mouth publicity.

Thus, from a happy and loyal customer, you will turn into an ambassador or promoter of my books. If I continue to add value to your business/profession, you will benefit and be successful in your area of work. I will get more business and "Will Win With You."

I am sure that by this time you would have realized the importance of keeping customers interested. I will explain how we can keep our customers interested. But before that let me expand our approach. What happens to customers psychologically when they are interested? They experience a certain degree of excitement, which is a good experience. Excitement is one of the good emotions we would like customers to have, but that is not enough. There are many more positive emotions we would like to trigger to create a delightful customer experience through the 5 stages of the customer journey. This brings us to an important topic of customer experience creation. Keeping things interesting is an integral part of customer experience and thus, I will talk about customer experience first.

Customer Experience and its Management

Customer experience is nothing but how customers feel while dealing with you. What ultimate impression customers carry of you is customer experience. Let's understand it with a short scenario. Rohan works in an architectural firm and after the end of the day, he is supposed to purchase vegetables for himself. He has two options giving two different experiences to meet this need.

Experience 1 is that after leaving the office he goes to a nearby local market. He reaches the market and starts searching for a space to park his car as the local market lanes are narrow. He finds a spot nearby and starts walking towards the market. The roads are busy with shoppers and vehicles.

He reaches a vendor and asks, "How much for 1 Kg of ladyfinger?"

Vendor says, "60 rupees a Kg."

Rohan asks, "Final Price?"

The vendor replies, "Yes sir, 60 is the rate. But out of respect for you, I will give for 55."

Rohan says, "Okay," and takes the vegetable. After crossing a few shops, he hears someone shouting and selling, "Ladyfinger, Rs. 40 a Kg." Rohan thought it must be a stale lot, that's why he is selling it for such a low price. Going further, he sees some good quality ladyfinger at another shop and asks the rate. To his surprise, this was selling at 40 rupees a Kg. Nevertheless, he continued purchasing.

After this experience, he started bargaining hard with sellers and at some places had to hear, "Sir, this is the final rate. If you want it, take it. Else do not waste my time."

Still, he continued until the bags were full and became quite heavy. It so happened that it started drizzling and he had to take shelter in a local shop for 10 mins. After the rain stopped, he took his bags and left for the parking spot.

Experience 2 is where Rohan decides to go to a mall that is on the way to his home. He parks the vehicle in secured parking by paying parking charges and enters the mall. He is greeted politely at entry by the security guard who did a security check as well. He goes to the fruit and vegetable section of a well-known hypermarket. There, he picks up a trolley and finds a section well-maintained with price tags being put on all the vegetables. There is no restriction on the minimum quantity to be bought. The section is air conditioned with a nice aroma. After the vegetable purchase is done, he picks up a box of chocolate for his nephew on the way out. He uses the express lane and pays the bill quickly. He carries the trolley to the car, shifts purchases, and leaves the mall. By the way, the ladyfinger was priced at Rs. 50 a Kg here but he could redeem some of his coupons/parking tickets while billing.

You can imagine now how two experiences are different. What do you think? Which experience Rohan would like to repeat? The majority of us will answer that experience-2 was better. The reason for this answer is also obvious because the mall experience is better for a person like Rohan. Despite a little additional expense, he would like to opt for a better experience. That is the power of creating an experience. **Customers will be willing to pay a premium if the experience is worth it. They will not only pay more but they will repeat the purchase as well.**

So, how do we create a delightful experience for customers? Under **Task 9 of Chapter 5**, you would have done the following:

a. Mapping your customer journey under the 5 Stages of awareness, consideration, decision, retention, and advocacy.

b. Identifying possible touch points under 5 stages.

Keeping the above in mind, you need to observe and experience **the customer's life throughout the 5 stages.** What I mean is that you will have to take each stage one by one and observe every detail of what customers go through in that stage. You will also have to note down what customers see, feel, touch, smell, and taste during the journey. Then you can identify changes that can be made to improve the customers' experience in each stage. Let me illustrate with an example where a customer is at the retention stage (which means he is using the offering) of having a stay at a holiday resort.

Illustration -

What Customers Go Through	Customer Experience	How can Experience be Enhanced
Resorts with similar-sounding names were in the same vicinity. Thus, it took some time to find the place. Asked locals about the address.	Inconvenient navigation, confusion, and time-consuming. When locals don't know the place, it seems the place may not be that good.	Suitable boards and directional signboards. Proactive sharing of location on the map. Unique branding along the way with distance mentioned.

Continued...

Security check at the main gate. Name, contact details, etc. are filled in a register and security confirms by calling reception.	Entering details and cross-checking by security is all right as long as it does not take much time. Neutral feeling.	What if security is given a list of guests expected to arrive each day and only by giving their names, customers get a warm welcome?
The customer arrives at the reception area. There is space for seating, the lobby is double heightened with attractive interiors. Many people are waiting for their turn and are taken care of. Welcome drink is served. Staff is looking busy managing the check-ins.	Good feeling about the resort. Liked the welcome drink and felt refreshed. Feeling good that the family is getting a chance to take a good selfie. Many people are still waiting and being in line for check-in triggers a feeling of a race where customers feel that he/she should get started as early as possible.	Based on rush hour analysis provision of additional staff to support faster check-in. An assuring system of a first-come-first-serve basis for calling out names to come forward for the check-in process so that customers need not stand in line.

Continued...

Chapter 6 Keeping Them Interested

Inside the room, the customer finds all the required information for usage of the room and services. All equipment, wi-fi, etc. are working fine. The customer calls reception and notes down what can be explored in the resort.	Feeling excellent. No complaints. Sets up a good mood to start with.	If a small takeaway guide showcases what attractions the resort offers with timing, fee, and with some pictures placed in the room, the family can plan their day better. Information on nearby sightseeing locations will enable them to explore more things while going back. This may create a wow factor for many customers.

Continued...

While using the indoor games room, the attendees were very cooperative and polite. However, at the swimming pool, people were non-responsive and service was slow.	Positive and felt respected in the indoor games room but at the pool did not get a good experience. Had to be assertive with one of the staff.	Regular training on soft skills for all people across the facility. Focus on service and customers has to be the same across. Supervisors observing sections regularly will help improve quality.
At the time of checkout, the customer brings all the luggage to the reception, submits the key, settles the bill, and leaves	As this is a practice at many places, customers feel all right. In their mind, relaxation time has come to an end.	If the resort proactively offers the same level of service during check-out as it offered during check-in, the customer will remember it as a positive surprise.

The above illustration is at a very broad level. When you are doing this exercise for your business/profession, you need to go into greater detail. Now, let us talk about some ways to keep customers interested and engaged to create a delightful customer experience.

Get the Basics Right

No one can continue to have a long successful business if the core product/service is not good and does not address customers' pains or gains. Only having a good marketing strategy or false propaganda is not going to help. The majority of providers (sellers) fail to put in place a robust customer-centric post-sales service system. That is one area where your sympathizer can convert into your promoter. I have already talked about the use of customers' complaints for enhancing the value offered to customers in previous chapters.

Go Beyond

A most delightful instance for customers is when they get more than what was expected or committed by the provider. What is committed is needed but if someone does a bit more, human beings feel satisfied. However, there is a risk involved. The more often you go beyond your commitment to customers as a policy, the customers' expectations of you go up. Based on their experience, they start expecting you to deliver more than your commitment every time. What should we do then? Confused? For me, every risk comes with an opportunity. Say your service and approach policy is 'going beyond', and the same is not provided by your competitors, customers understand the difference between you and your competitors. This is the time to check if you can command an advantage over your competitors. Informed customers will be willing to pay you more if they are assured and satisfied with your offering. However, you have to be cautious about the maximum level of premium which will be viable for the customer. You also have to know how many customers will be ready to pay the premium and if that fits into your business viability. That is where a conscious balance has to be maintained.

Continuous Engagement

Customer engagement is a great way to create a bond with your customers. There can be many occasions like wishing on birthdays/anniversaries, festivals, the launch of a new office/product, celebration of days of national importance, involvement in social work (CSR), etc. You may decide a practical logic on how and whom to engage. A simple example can be defining your key customer and engaging actively with them. Engagement activity can be designed as per customer categories and subcategories we saw in Chápter 2.

Bring Freshness

Change is the only constant in the world. Everyone gets interested in something new. Remember the "Breaking News" concept in Telemedia. When we hear the word

"Breaking News," automatically the attention and interest go up. We stop at the channel to know What is Breaking and Who is Breaking it. Similarly, when a provider launches a new scheme, product, feature, or look, the buyer gets interested. Yes, it is more relevant for the B2C (Business to Customer) category but even in the case of B2B (Business to Business) or individual professionals, positive fresh changes are noticed. A refurbished office, new brochure, flexible payment option, new payment mode and support service are all good ways to keep the customer interested. However, just like how "Breaking News' has lost its original importance due to over-leveraging without substance, our freshness cannot be for the sake of it. It has to be initiated with due reason and thought process.

Rewards

Having a reward system is a great way to keep customers interested. Rewards can be based on many criteria:

(a) Having a random draw from all the customers and offering a percentage of discount on the next buy. This happens all the time when you visit a mall.
(b) Loyalty reward which is based on repeat business in the form of a discount on a second purchase or a bundled offering.

(c) Referral rewards when a customer brings in friends or family and they engage in business with us.
(d) Instant reward in form of cashback or redeemable reward points
(e) Opportunity for kids/family members to win rewards by participating in quizzes/competitions which may or may not be related to your offering.

Design Details

The more we observe customer activity in detail (as suggested in the illustration at the start of the chapter), the better customer/end-user experience we can create. In fact, smaller gestures create more delight for customers. When you do the illustrated exercises for yourselves, you will find out many areas where you can improve the customer experience.

Customer Exit

Generally, you will not find many people talking about the phase where customers exit. That is why this phase is mostly neglected and left to untrained staff who are supposed to ensure formal closure only. According to me, handling customer exit is important from two aspects:

(1) Customer exit (or Customer choosing not to go with you) may happen due to various reasons which may or may not be in our control. There are many factors

that a customer considers before making a decision. That is why giving due respect to the customer's decision and trying to know the reasons for the decision is important. It will allow us to know where we can improve in the future, which might help reduce further exits.

(2) If a customer has a bitter experience while exiting, they will influence other potential customers through word-of-mouth. If we provide a decent and respectful exit, it shows our professional approach towards customers. Exiting on a good note also keeps the window open for customers to return to you in the future.

Measure and Improve Customer Experience

I have explained customer feedback and the use of customer feedback outcomes in detail in Chapters 3 and 4 respectively. Measuring the customer experience is an extension of the same approach. For measuring the experience, questions and forms of responses can be modified. A well-known and popular measure of experience is **the Net Promoter Score' (NPS).**

To calculate NPS, customers are simply asked how likely they are to recommend you to a friend, on a scale of 0-10. Scores 0-6 are detractors, scores 7-8 are passives, and scores 9-10 are promoters. NPS is the percentage of detractor responses subtracted from promoter responses.

With NPS, we can instantly tell how many customers are happy enough with their customer experience that they have become ambassadors for your brand.

As I mentioned earlier, for a better customer feedback program, professional assistance should be taken, if financially viable.

Let's conclude Chapter - 6 in form of the **reader's tasks.**

Task 12: Actions to Enhance Customer Experience

In line with the illustrative table, identify the probable actions you can take for all the 5 stages customers go through. Think of yourself as a customer and be empathetic while doing this exercise. Also, try to incorporate pleasant surprises for customers to keep them interested. Relook at the customer engagement program as well.

Task 13: Study Customer Exit Analysis

See how you behave and treat customers when they exit. Evaluate if customers will be comfortable coming back to you if they wish to. Take the data from the last few years to understand why customers exited or did not buy from you. Do an appropriate analysis of data and see if some patterns or common reasons are appearing. If yes, those are the areas where you need to improve.

Chapter 7

Ahead of Competition

Today, we live in a world where competition has no limits. Every day, we hear about a new venture offering a better and unique product or a service. According to the Government of India's Ministry of Commerce and Industry, India has the 3rd largest startup ecosystem in the world. In a period of 5 years between Jan 2016 to Dec 2020, more than 41,000 startups were recognised in India. In the year 2020 alone, more than 14,000 startups were recognised. That means, on average, 20+ startups were recognised every day during these 5 years. This journey is expected to witness growth with consistent annual growth of 12-15%.

If you see on an individual professional's front, more than 15 Lakh engineers, 1 Lakh doctors, and 5 Lakh Lawyers pass out from their respective colleges every year. Not all of them start their venture, though. On the industrial front, approximately 5,000 new micro, small and medium enterprises (MSMEs) get registered every year. These numbers strongly indicate what kind of competition organizations and professionals are expected to face on a routine basis. The advancement and use of new technologies are offering a better experience to customers. Mobile applications, WhatsApp connect, Chatbot, online payments, auto-replies, etc. have become the norm. Customers consider these as basic nowadays. Customers experience and compare all the products/services they use during the day irrespective of the nature of the product/service. Did I say, "irrespective of nature?" Yes, and I mean it.

Let me explain. (a) Today, a customer who has experience with one-two day delivery through Amazon will be uncomfortable with a delivery period of 2 months for a two-wheeler. They may choose another comparable brand if it offers lesser waiting time. (b) With digital payment being accepted everywhere, if some shopkeeper asks for cash, he is seen as either rudimentary or trying to save tax. (c) Home delivery is welcome even from technicians for the repair of smaller equipment. I can't think of any product which is not offered to be delivered to your doorstep, at least in metropolitan and major cities. (d) Rude behaviour by any staff of a government organization is posted on social media like any other bad experience.

Chapter 7 Ahead of Competition

The need of the hour is to first understand what experience our customers are experiencing and liking. These experiences can be from our competitors or some unrelated product and service. Then, work on providing a similar experience to customers throughout the 5 customer journey stages for our product/service. To understand and learn from competitors or other unrelated product/service offerings, we need to adopt a proven approach called **benchmarking.**

What is Benchmarking

By definition, benchmarking is the practice of comparing business processes and performance metrics to industry bests and best practices from other companies.

Simply put, it is seeing our practices and performance against those who are better than us. The purpose of benchmarking is to learn and improve. We can categorize Benchmarking under **three categories (Cat.)** based on the impact they can have on the business:

Cat. 1: System Benchmarking	This is the highest level of benchmarking. Here, we compare strategy, business model, culture, governance, emerging trends, purpose, etc.
Cat. 2: Process Benchmarking	This is the second level of benchmarking. Here, we compare function-specific processes like sales, marketing, communication, customer relationship management, employee care, purchase, post-sales, etc. In-depth studies of these end-to-end processes are done so that we can identify which stage(s) of the process needs improvement. For example, an end-to-end marketing process can have stages like identification of target customer group, identification of USP and value proposition, identification of communication media and messages, innovative and interesting marketing campaign, events and promotions, use of brand ambassadors, potential customer engagement, monitoring of response and course correction, etc.

Continued...

Cat. 3: Performance Benchmarking	Here, we look at the quantifiable performance which is comparable. Each sector has certain metrics/measures which are used by all the players. For example, the financial performance of the companies is compared on revenue (topline), profit (bottom line), working capital ratio, debt to equity, price to earnings ratio, return on equity, etc. More than learning, the purpose of performance benchmarking is to compare outcomes. Improvement in outcomes can be done through improvement in the corresponding process.

Let us understand how these categories are **interlinked**. If I ask how you will know if you are better than your competitors who are eying the same customer group as you. For this, we will have to compare your performance metrics (measures), with the competitors' performance. There can be many comparable measures but the key measures will be in the area of financial results and customer results. We will try to get the correct data and put the results like the table below:

Measure	Own Performance	Competitor 1	Competitor 2
Revenue (Cr)	500	350	600
Revenue Growth over last year (%)	8%	10%	20%
Profit (Cr)	75	56	60
Profit % of Revenue	15%	16%	10%
New Subscriber (%)	5%	6%	22%

From the above table, we will realize that we are at par with the first competitor, however, the second competitor is better at acquiring new subscribers in the last year which might have resulted in better growth of revenue. However, the percentage of profit for Competitor 2 is lower than that for us and Competitor 1. It is a possibility that Competitor 2 is passing on discounts or spending more on marketing to acquire new customers.

What we did just now is performance benchmarking with competitors as a sample. When we add all our key competitors in the above table then this benchmarking will be completed.

Now, coming back to the use of this performance benchmarking (Cat.3). As per your business plans and strategy you will choose which measure is more important for you, and where you want to be ahead of your competition. Let's say you want to have a better subscriber (customer) base than all your competitors. However, performance benchmarking says that you have not done well on this count. To understand what your competitor is doing better, you need to do process benchmarking (Cat.2) for the processes which help you get more subscribers. The processes can be marketing, sales, new product development, customer referral, etc. You will understand where your related processes need improvement and should initiate the changes based on this process benchmarking. This is how Cat.3 benchmarking is connected with Cat. 2 benchmarking.

Suppose during the process benchmarking (Cat.2) you realize that there are huge gaps in multiple processes which are impacting your desired outcome. In this scenario, you may have to do Cat.1 (system) benchmarking with a best-in-class company to bring in fundamental and big changes in the way you operate. You may realize that despite improving operational processes your achieved results are not in-line with the expected outcome. In that case, you may need to do system benchmarking (Cat.1) for your strategy, business model, operating segment, etc.

Many times, for complete transformation, companies start with Cat. 1 benchmarking, for example, to set up their purpose, long-term vision, and direction. Post that they further design the process and measure with an adequate Cat. 2 and Cat. 3 benchmarking.

Whom to Benchmark With

I believe that learning has no boundaries and a core reason for benchmarking is to learn and improve. It will be incorrect to limit benchmarking to our direct competitors alone. That is the reason we need to have a robust and comprehensive structure of benchmarking. I will explain a model which you can adopt. In this model, we will bifurcate benchmarking based on the entities we are comparing ourselves to. This model is successfully deployed by Godrej Construction in real life. In fact, in their model, they have one more layer between BM 0 and BM 1, where they compare themselves with other strategic business units of their parent company Godrej & Boyce Mfg. Co. Ltd.

Chapter 7 Ahead of Competition

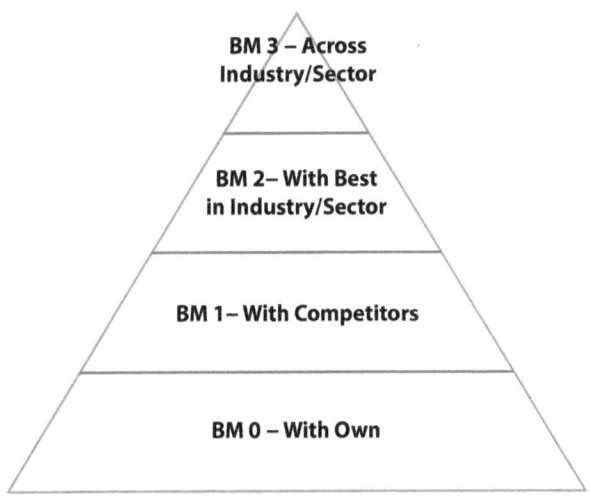

BM 0 is revisiting our own practices, checking our past performance, and seeing where we are today. This allows us to see past trends and set the right targets for the future.

BM 1 is comparing ourselves with our direct competitors. Ideally, all the key competitors should be considered, however, the top 3 competitors are also sufficient.

BM 2 is comparing ourselves with the best of our sector/industry. They may not be competing with us but are trend setters and successful in the same industry. For example, I may be running a hostel for working people, but I can still do a process benchmark with Airbnb (an online marketplace for short-term homestays). Another one is that I run a bus travel agency, still, I can do a system/process benchmark with Vistara (an airline) as we are operating in the same industry.

BM 3 is crossing over to any other industry/sector and comparing ourselves with the best. Generally, it is more relevant for Cat. 2 (process) benchmarking. For example, an auto manufacturing company can process benchmark with Amazon's delivery and tracking system. Another example is that cab aggregators can process benchmark vendor development with auto manufacturers. Even an A.C. repair company can process benchmark its technician reward program with the cab aggregator partner reward program. There are functions and processes which are common to almost every organization like HR, purchase, safety, IT, etc. These processes are the best candidates for BM 3.

Task 14: Set a benchmarking process for yourself.

Please use categories (Cat. 1 to Cat. 3) and benchmarking models (BM 0 to BM 3) to establish your own benchmarking process and implement the same. While you do the benchmarking, give special attention to the enabling technology being used by others. A judicious review and adoption of new technology can benefit you immensely.

Chapter 7 Ahead of Competition

Certification, Awards & Competitions

In my opinion, participating in all sorts of certifications, awards and competitions is a great form of benchmarking. When we go for any certification or accreditation, we are expected to follow certain criteria set by the respective body. In order to get the accreditation/certification we have to demonstrate proof of implementation as per their qualifying criteria. Qualified persons check the implementation and give their observations. If we meet the criteria, we are certified. If not, we have to make improvements and attempt again. Almost all certifications and accreditation come with a validity period. Periodic audits/assessments are carried out. This continual process helps us maintain the required level and acts as a reassurance to customers. The most reliable and universally acceptable certifications are the ones offered by ISO (International Organization for Standardization). ISO is an independent, non-governmental and international organization with a membership of 167 national standard bodies. Through its members, it brings together experts to share knowledge and develop voluntary, consensus-based, market-relevant international standards that support innovation and provide solutions to global challenges.

Today, ISO offers more than 24,000 international standards covering almost all aspects of technology, management, and manufacturing. There are generic ones like ISO 9001 for quality, ISO 14001 for the environment, ISO 45001 for safety, ISO 50001 for energy management, ISO 27001 for information security, etc. And there are industry-specific ones like ISO 13485 for medical devices, ISO 22000 for food safety, ISO 13216 for child seats for cars, etc.

Similarly, there are government-recognised accreditation bodies that operate in their respective areas. For example, the National Board of Accreditation (NBA) for Higher education institutes, the Distance Education Council (DEC) for regulating distance education, the National Accreditation Board for Hospitals & Healthcare Providers (NABH), etc.

You can evaluate which certification/accreditation is relevant for you and will help you to either improve customer aspects or production aspects.

Coming to awards and competitions. When we apply for any award/competition, we are first supposed to submit what we have done which is better than others. Then, our claim is evaluated by a neutrally experienced jury/assessor. Experienced assessors can ask the right questions and see things from different perspectives. If taken in the right spirit, we are bound to benefit from this exercise. I have the experience of participating in some of the awards and have witnessed the benefit it brings to the organization.

Chapter 7 Ahead of Competition

One of those awards was CII Customer Obsession Award and the other was CII-EXIM Award for Business Excellence. Both of these awards are based on a predefined model and expect us to first learn and implement the model followed by participating in the award process. During the award process, we need to submit our self-assessment report describing how well we have implemented the model. Assessment of our submission is done by a group of competent professionals and at the end of the assessment, they provide us with a detailed report. The report talks about our strengths and areas where we need improvement. If taken with the right mindset, this report can trigger business transformation.

The history of the **Confederation of Indian Industry (CII)** is a story of the transformation of a minuscule association, representing a small segment of the industry, to the premier business association of modern India. CII's primary goal is to develop the Indian industry and to ensure that the government and society as a whole, understand both the needs of the industry and its contribution to the nation's wellbeing. It has many specialized centres of excellence to cater to the needs of almost every sector, for example, the CII Institute of Quality, CII Institute of Logistics, CII-ITC Centre of Excellence for Sustainable Development, CII Centre of Excellence for Innovation, Entrepreneurship and

Start-ups, etc. These centres promote excellence through awards and competitions as well.

Participating and getting recognition binds the employees to a common cause and promotes healthy competition. Winning team or individual awards becomes motivating and can also attract customers.

While adopting the certification/award route, there are a **few suggestions** I would like to give to my readers:

(i) Do not be driven by wanting to receive many certificates/awards to such an extent that the opportunity for improvements offered by the process is missed.

(ii) Always participate in reliable and fair competitions.

(iii) Prefer an award that recommends an improvement model to be adopted for assessment.

(iv) Align your entire team by explaining the reason and benefits of the certification/accreditation.

(v) Merge the requirements with routine work so that it is not a standalone effort.

(vi) Communicate the benefits received regularly.

(vii) Most importantly, do not do this for namesake. Do it whole heartedly.

Task 15: Identify relevant certifications or awards/competitions.

Please go through the websites of ISO, CII, and respective industry/professional associations. Considering the best fit for your strategy and what your customers may find valuable, make the choice.

Data to Decision

We all know that in this fiercely competitive world, every decision we take can impact the business adversely. Every decision we take carries risk and thus, decisions based on gut feeling are not reliable anymore. Availability of data and information is in abundance and with digital enhancement, the entire world has become one platform. In earlier chapters and tasks, I suggested you to gather data and information about customers. I mentioned that the more granular you go, the better it is. But the million-dollar question is, what do we do with data? The data and information will be available to your competitor as well. So, with this level playing field how to be ahead of the competition?

The answer lies in a **data analytics-based decision-making approach.** In this approach, I need not tell you how to decide because that depends on various variables and you are the best person to decide for yourself. The point I want you to consider is the use of data analytics for making decisions. Today, data analytics has become a science in itself and requires a greater depth of study, but I can give you some basic understanding here:

(a) What is Data

Data is a collection of facts, statistics, and information that is either quantitative or qualitative. It can be in the form of numbers, words, images, or any other representation of information. Earlier people defined data as pure numbers and organized data as information. However, now the line is blurred and data is considered from a broader perspective as mentioned here.

(b) Insights and knowledge

Data is used to gain insights and knowledge. By analysing data, businesses can identify patterns and trends that can help them to optimize their operations, improve efficiency, and identify growth opportunities.

(c) Informed Decision

A balanced and informed decision is possible when insights and knowledge from different aspects are considered together. Decision options can be evaluated with associated pros and cons. This allows you to reduce the unknown risks of any decision. Whereas, known risks can be addressed in time.

(d) Key Benefits

Data can give businesses a competitive edge by enabling them to identify new markets, develop better products and services, and tailor their offerings to meet the needs of their customers. Data can be used to gain insights into customer behaviour and preferences, allowing businesses to provide a more personalized and tailored experience. This can help to improve customer satisfaction and drive customer loyalty. Data can be used to optimize business processes and reduce waste, leading to improved efficiency and lower costs. Overall, data is an important resource that can help businesses to make better decisions, gain a competitive edge, and drive growth.

(e) Types of Data Analytics

(e1) Descriptive analytics is a type of data analysis that summarizes data to understand what has happened in the past. **For example,** suppose you work for a retail company that sells clothing, and you want to understand the sales trends of a particular product in the last year. To perform descriptive analytics on this data, you might start by calculating some basic statistics, such as the mean, median, and mode of the daily sales figures. This would give you an idea of the typical sales volume and revenue generated on a given day/week/month, which can be visualized through line charts or bar graphs. This will show how the sales figures have varied over time and allow you to identify trends or patterns in the data such as whether sales have been increasing or decreasing over the last six months.

(e2) Diagnostic analytics focuses on identifying the root cause of a problem by analysing historical data. It uses data mining techniques to identify patterns, correlations, and anomalies in data to provide insights into why something happened. Taking the **same example forward,** for the retail store you notice that sales have decreased in the last month. By visualising and looking at patterns and trends, you might notice that sales for a particular product category have dropped significantly or that sales from a specific campaign have decreased. Based on your analysis and with the help of appropriate tools like Why-Why, Fishbone, Pareto Chart, etc. you can identify the root cause of the problem. You discover that a recent change in your pricing strategy led to a decrease in sales. Now that you have identified the problem, you can take corrective action to address it. In this case, you might adjust your pricing strategy, launch a new campaign, or offer promotions to incentivize customers to purchase from your store again.

(e3) Predictive analytics is a branch of data analytics that uses statistical models and machine learning algorithms to analyse data and make predictions about future events

Chapter 7 Ahead of Competition

or behaviours. It could be used to predict whether a customer is likely to purchase a product based on their past behaviour and demographic information. Let's say your dataset has customer information, including their age, gender, past purchases, and whether they have subscribed to your social media page. Using this dataset, you could build a predictive model to determine the likelihood of a customer making a purchase. The model will consider the customer's age, gender, location, past purchase history, and whether they have engaged with your recent marketing efforts. Accordingly, this model would generate a prediction of whether the customer is likely to purchase in the near future or not. You can use this prediction to develop targeted marketing campaigns aimed at customers who are most likely to make a purchase, which could include personalized email offers or social media ads which are tailored to the individual customer's preferences and behaviour.

To sum up Chapter 7, continuous learning and improvement are the only way forward for any organization or professional to be ahead of its competition. Benchmarking, adoption of continuous improvement systems, participation in value-adding awards and competitions, use of appropriate technology, and adopting data-based decision-making are key to success.

Chapter 8

Winning Together

In all the previous chapters we have been talking about 'customer's win' and how best a provider can help customers in winning. But then, is success ensured if only these two entities are working towards the same goal? Probably not. Like in the game of soccer. Everybody knows where to put the ball. Still, can one or two people win a game by playing in sync with only each other while out of sync with the rest of the team?

No, the entire team of forwards, midfielders, and defenders need to work together. If the midfielder forgets the goal position, he is bound to pass the ball in the wrong direction and maybe to the wrong team. The goalkeeper and defenders have to be alert so that the other team (competition) does not get away with the goal. The passing of the ball has to be well coordinated so that their club/ owner/country (customer) wins as intended. They all can play because the Club/ Owner/ country is paying for the team. If the club does not win, players will not win any

Chapter 8 Winning Together

name, fame, or money. They have a customer-provider relationship where soccer-playing skills are provided as a service to the club. Now think of the tournaments as the territory you are currently playing in. There are many more territories to capture if you are capable and willing.

The playing field is your area of operation, and the referees are the government and statutory bodies who tell you how to operate. If there is no foul, the game continues, if any rule is broken you have to pay a penalty. The captain of the soccer team is like the leader of the organization or proprietor in the case of a smaller firm. He guides, motivates, encourages, and plays his part actively in the functioning of the team. But because he is too involved in the game and is expected to play his own role, the manager and support staff are hired. The manager is an experienced non-playing person who is responsible for player management and in-game coaching.

To me, the job of the manager is like management systems for an organization. Systems like ISO Management Systems and Enterprise resource planning (ERP) include processes, structure, dos and don'ts, flow, guidelines, etc. Then comes the coach of the team. The coach is more focused on team preparation, practices, and training the players in the best possible manner to win matches. He makes strategies and plans for the team along with the manager and captain. In a business context as well, many times we take the help of internal/external coaches and facilitators for strategy formulation, training, and capability building. There are proven methods that are widely used.

While making strategy, this group of the coach, manager, and captain, consider all the data and information available to them about their team and competing team. They also consider factors beyond their control like weather, quality of ground, etc. They see the availability of resources like which player is fit and ready, which department is weaker/stronger, what are the substitute options, what is the past performance of the team, etc. Then, they work out various possible options of attack in terms of when to accelerate, what route to take, and who can score. The most suitable strategy is finalized and communicated to all the team members so that they know their roles. During the match, if some part of the game plan does not work, the decision-making group comes together and changes the plan as per the circumstances. This is nothing but agile strategic course correction.

In case of a lost game, the core reason/root cause is identified so that the team does not repeat mistakes in the next game. One lost game or one bad day does not make the team bad. Another day, another opportunity will come soon if you are willing to improve yourself. The same is the case with business. If you have lost ground somewhere, be open to unlearning and learning.

Chapter 8 Winning Together

Understand where you need to improve to win back customers and retain them for life. The more you achieve wins for your customer, the more faith the customer will develop in you and you will surely get more business. That is the whole idea of **"Winning with Your Customer."**

Three important things are understood from the analogy of the soccer field:

1. The ultimate aim is customer winning
2. Your strategy should support you to get to this aim, and
3. The entire team, all players need to be working in alignment with the same strategy

About the first point of ultimate aim, I have already written a lot. In fact, the entire book is about how to make your customer a winner. So, assuming that there is no doubt left in the minds of readers that our aim should be towards this cause, I want to touch upon the other 2 points in a little detail.

The second point is Supporting Strategy. The formulation of a strategy is to meet the end goal; it is not a new concept. There are many established principles and explanations which are available and the majority of us know about them. So, I will not elaborate much on the process. But with customer focus in mind, I am formulating a simple-to-understand flow chart. The below chart highlights various concepts talked about in the book and can be considered a customer-focused strategy flow. This will apply to all businesses and professionals, except the level of detailing and variables involved may be different.

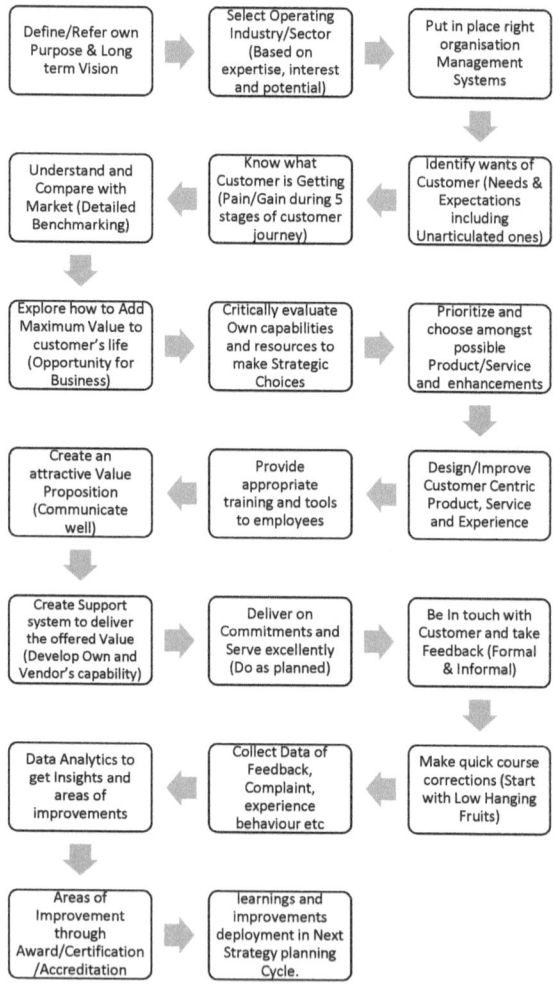

Chapter 8 Winning Together

One important aspect of implementing the customer-focused strategy is to track it properly. People may be highly enthusiastic and vocal during strategy formulation meetings. But there is a good possibility that once the routine works are back, they tend to overlook these new strategies. To address this, you can adopt a model where these new strategies are implemented through smaller projects. These projects will have a structured approach to planning, assigning responsibility, and monitoring. Let's see how the projects can be identified. Assuming you are in the business of packaged flavored milk:

Strategy	Possible Projects	Who Should Lead It
Add 3 new flavors to the product, offering and increase the sale by 10% from new flavors in the next 2 years. (This might have come from the last customer survey where customers said you offer limited flavors)	**Project 1: Market research to identify 5-6 flavors that customers may like within 3 months** (This will include consumer research, consumption pattern, benchmarking with competitors & chocolate industry, prioritized list of flavors, etc.)	Marketing supported by R&D

Continued...

	Project 2: Identification of new customers or geographic segments which are likely to purchase new flavors. (This will include field trials, business potential and financial viability analysis, price discovery, etc.)	Business Development Team
	Project 3: Production capability analysis considering the expected sale from new flavors in XYZ months. (This will include data analytics on production trends, capacity utilization, throughput, vendor capacity check, new vendor tie-up, new production facility provision, etc.)	Supply Chain Management Team
	Project 4: Launch and marketing strategy for new flavors by XYZ month. (This will include USP identification, target group-based campaign, brand ambassador, promotional events, etc.)	Marketing and Communication Team

Ideally, the above 4 projects should be identified at the time of the strategy formulation meeting itself so that work can be started. Below are some of the features you should consider while formulating the project. Please remember that the format of the project is not important, but the content of the project is very important.

I. **The name** of the project should give a very clear idea about what we are trying to achieve through the project. Keeping a generic heading dampens the drive to finish the project. Adding a finite target in terms of time, cost, revenue, or any other number is advisable.

II. **The purpose** of the project should be mentioned because it brings back the larger strategic goal in focus. All the teams working on different projects must know that they are contributing to the larger plan and their failure is going to impact the organization's plan.

III. **The outcomes** of the project are important to identify. These should not only be the result measures but also the measures which are expected in between (lead indicators). The outcome should ideally pass the test of SMART (specific, measurable, achievable, relevant, and time-bound)

IV. **Individual Roles** in the project should be clear. In the structure, you must have one key person who will drive the entire project as a leader. He can be supported by a senior guide and colleagues/juniors as team members. It is important to also specify the role of each of the team members who are a part of the project. The role should also reflect in the individual performance planning and review system.

V. **Risks and alternative** plans should be identified in case something goes wrong. This is done to know the cost of failure and how we can best face the situation caused by a failure.

VI. **Reviewing** with a periodic set frequency is the most important task for the success of the project. Review frequency and at what level review must happen depends upon the project's criticality and duration. Still, a fortnightly review with the team lead and a monthly review with the business leaders can be a good benchmark. The measures for the review should be chosen carefully as measurement drives behaviour.

VII. **Celebrating** success is one mantra a good leader always follows. The same should be applied and people should be recognised for the successful completion of the projects.

VIII. **Embracing** failure is a virtue we must have, especially in projects where we are trying and experimenting with something new. Many times, challenging projects are taken to stretch the teams for the better. Thus, failure in such projects should be acceptable if sufficient effort is demonstrated.

IX. **Learning** is the last step of a completed project. It must be captured in both successful and failed projects. This data captured over time will become valuable insights for the organization

The above key features have been identified from my own experience with Godrej Construction (Award Winner of the CII-EXIM Award for Business Excellence 2021 and 2022). I was fortunate to work in the Business Strategy formulation and Deployment team. I also steered a special group of customers at Godrej Construction. As a group, our job was to go through the analysis of all customer-related processes like customer buying patterns, lost deal data, conversions, emerging behavior, customer formal feedback, customer verbatims, informal inputs, customer complaints, referrals, recommendations, benchmarking, competition data, etc. Based on analysis and patterns emerging from the above processes we used to identify the Improvement areas and projects for each LoB and division. Our work was validated and further improved by the respective LoBs based on their analysis. Finally, customer strategy and supporting projects were formulated and approved by seniors.

Over the years customer-focused strategy and improvement projects have helped Godrej Construction immensely. Under the 3rd party customer satisfaction study their customer satisfaction index has been moving up consistently and as of the year 2022 (FY 22-23) all of their LoBs **have moved above 87 with the highest LoB at 93**. Even on Net Promoter Scores (NPS), all their LoBs are going very strong and their **score is above 70 with the highest LoB at 89.**

Net Promoter Score (NPS) is a measure used to gauge customer loyalty, satisfaction, and enthusiasm with a company that's calculated by asking customers one question: "On a scale from 0 to 10, how likely are you to recommend this product/company to a friend or colleague? Generally, an NPS score between 30 to 70 is considered 'great', and above 70 is considered to be 'excellent.'

To take the analogy "Winning with Your Customer" forward, let me show you how progress on customer delight ensures business progress as well. While Godrej Construction moved ahead on customer-focused practices and improved on customer feedback, they also improved their business performance. For more than the last 5-6 years, they have been surpassing their topline (revenue) and bottom line (profit) consistently. To give a specific correlation between customer focus and business performance I would like to give an example of LoB Construction Materials. This LoB provides various construction materials, predominantly ready-mix concrete (RMC) to its customers. The main product of this business is like a commodity and switching cost for customers is almost NIL. Competition is also tough from established and local players.

Despite that, this LoB continued their focus on making their customer win. They took more than 15-20 big-ticket changes, having a positive impact on customers. These changes were in different areas like new product introduction, service enhancement, communication and tracking, on-site services, customer care center, mobile applications, branding and visibility, appearance, product co-development, intermediate feedback, complaint monitoring and analysis etc.

By bringing these changes between FY18-19 to FY22-23, their customer satisfaction index improved from 80 to 92 whereas their **NPS improved from 35 to 70.** In the same period, their **revenue grew by 118%** whereas the **profit increased to 142%**. Except for one Covid year aberration both revenue and profit are in consistent growth mode. During this period, they have grown with a CAGR of more than 20% YOY. With the achievement of new heights in customer feedback they are also getting rewarded in financial terms. Both their customers and they are winning together.

I have no doubt that if an organization implements the "Win with Your Customer" approach in the right spirit, it will be successful financially. I believe that readers would have got good insights on strategy formulation and implementation and thus, it is time for a task to implement the learnings.

Task 16: Strategy Formulation and Supporting Project

The readers will relook into their existing practices and improve the same based on the flow chart I have created. The readers will implement at least one strategic goal through supporting projects immediately. Comprehensive changes can be made from the next year's strategy cycle.

Coming to the third important point from the soccer analogy, about all players working for the same strategy-

Like the soccer example, in business also, we need to align all the people and entities who directly or indirectly support us in meeting the customer goals. In business, the players are employees, suppliers, vendors, partners, associates, distributors, agents, consultants, etc. All these players need to be aligned with the strategy and supporting projects.

There can be two ways for this alignment. **The first**, which is to communicate directly, is very easy. You talk about the importance of customer focus again and again with them. You send them to training and seminars for learning. This is required but has limitations in getting the results consistently. Because although people will understand the importance, they may not put in their full effort because the model looks voluntary and slow-moving. In the case of external parties, they will have their priorities and thus any voluntary model is avoidable. Smaller partners/suppliers will not understand what exactly is to be done by them.

Thus, the second way is to communicate in writing. Needless to say, written communication becomes binding on the parties and thus it is best to give customers specific points in the contract or job description. While doing so, you may also decide on different levels of commitment and support needed by different entities. For example, a design consultant will need to be in much more in sync with customer needs and expectations than a stationary supplier.

Putting a condition for franchise owners, to ensure familiar customer experience across the world, is not new. You will find a similar look and feel in stores of McDonald's, Croma, Walmart, and Decathlon anywhere across the cities. The majority of auto companies prescribe the minimum area and facilities for the customer in all their service centres like reception, washrooms, and waiting rooms with TV, newspapers, magazines, etc. For vendors, lead time for all the supplies can be pre-defined with a delay penalty clause. To motivate and engage them positively, before-time delivery incentives can also be announced.

For employees – As an example, an employee's job description and performance evaluation criteria can talk about achieving a customer satisfaction score above 85%. It may be defined that their rating will depend on the percentage of the score they get from customers. The job description can specify that they need to create a customer engagement calendar and follow it more than 90% of the time.

Above are some anecdotal examples of measures. We need to systematically cascade the actions and measures across all the contributing players. We need to follow the common saying, **"If you can measure it, you can improve it"** and that is why cascading measures become very important. Let me illustrate the cascading exercise for you.

Illustration - The strategy may be implemented through special projects or routine work. In both cases, we need to know who is dependent on whom. For example, the head of the marketing team depends on and gets the field research work done through his/her subordinates. The subordinates depend upon an external agency to give them a list of people for consumer research. Appointment of this external agency is done by the procurement team.

Now suppose, the head of marketing wants to start the field research within a week, but his subordinates cannot do that because they do not have sufficient leads from the external agency. The agency is not providing further data because its contract with the company is not renewed. The procurement team can not renew their contract for another month. Ultimately, the research work is getting delayed which is impacting the launch of a new product for the company.

To avoid this scenario, implement one of the project features I mentioned above, i.e., talk about the involvement and commitment of different team members at the time of planning itself. The exercise of identifying the person responsible and the action needed as a continuous chain **from top to bottom is called cascading of actions.**

Establishing cascading of actions is a prerequisite for **cascading the deliverables or measures or performance indicators**.

Based on the actions cascading matrix, a table showing key measures coming out of those actions can be prepared. This table will contain all key measures which are critical and can be assigned as performance measures to the respective team/individual. An illustrative cascading is as below:

Measure for Head of Line of Business:
- New Product / Services - __ % of Revenue
- 100 % delivery on customer commitment
- Repeat business (70%)
- New Clients (30%)

Measure for Sales & Marketing Head:
- Launch of new paid service by Oct 2025
- Addressing customer issues (100% within SLA)
- Engagement with existing clients (No. of meetings, discussions, increase in wallet share, etc.)
- Number of interactions with prospective clients, the effectiveness of channel Partner / Agents

Measures for Business Development In charge: Market Analysis, Competition Analysis, Partner and Customer Analysis, etc. by May 2025, Business case approval by Jul 2025.

Measures for Customer Care In-charge: Adherence to SLA and % improvements, CAPA and reporting, Proper scheduling to ensure orders lost < 5%

Measures for Customer Relationship Manager: Adherence to Customer engagement calendar, Reporting market insights monthly, Competitor Mapping, Number / % of leads Converted into order, Revenue from New clients, Bagging 40% full project order

Continued...

Chapter 8 Winning Together

Measures for Customer Care Executive: Customer-wise delivery adherence >80%, Respond to Complaints within 4 hrs., Adequate communication to the customer on deviation

Measures for Customer Relationship Executive: Number of meetings with existing and new clients, area-wise list of new project launches and potential for business, Daily reporting in e-CRM, Update on sales scheme/incentive offered by competitors

Another Measure Cascading illustration on the Supplier side -

Measures for Head of Business:
- Performance against planned Financial Parameters (Profit as XYZ Cr., Operating Expenses as ABC Cr., etc.)
- Supplier Satisfaction Score (increase 15% YOY or 90%+)

Measures for Head of Purchase:
- Cost of material within or lower than budget
- Reduce the inventory carrying cost by 5% (BY Project on Just in Time)
- Enhance category-wise vendor based on 10% (Geography based)
- 100% milestones achievement on Vendor Feedback based Project

Continued...

> Measure for Purchase In-charge: 100% Delivery within Agreed SLA, Purchase within the approved budget, < 2 Quality issues within the year, 2X Alternate Vendor base, better credit terms than the industry
>
> Measure for Store In-charge: Efficient Inventory Management (No loss/ delay in production), Storage/pilferage loss <2%
>
> Measures for Purchase Executive: Development of category-wise vendor base in 3 months, Number of delays in releasing the payment to be less than 3%, Rating given by the supplier to be 8+ on all parameters.
>
> Measure for Store Executive – Zero stock out for critical materials, less than once a year for non-critical items.

Moving forward. Do you have absolute freedom to do what you want to do for customers? Or will your projects get implemented if proper cascading of actions and measures is done? Are we missing something?

Suppose you want to deliver pizza to a customer's house via drone and are ready to invest. Customers are also excited about this and are willing to pay a premium. You make all the marketing and launch plans. At the last moment, you realize that you cannot do this because as per government rules, one needs to take permission for using drones for any purpose, and delivery through drones is not allowed.

A live example of this situation is the bike taxi service (Transport service by two-wheeler) which is a unique and value-adding service for customers. It was started with high expectations of success by companies like Rapido, Ola, and Uber. However, soon after the launch, it was banned by many cities like Mumbai, Pune, and New Delhi citing different reasons. The matter is in the court of law and may ultimately be in favor of the aggregators with strict guidelines. But it has created hassles for the companies who have invested time, effort, and money.

In another situation, suppose you have initiated a one-on-one customer meeting plan with a tight timeline to finish. You are all geared up with identified team leads, team members, their schedules, questionnaires, the appointment of customers, etc. When you explain your plan to the team, you realize that one team member is getting married while another is going on maternity leave during the targeted timeline. Another one is already occupied with the promotion of a new product launch that happened last month. So, you have the project and cascading ready but a reduced team to implement it. You will have to either change the timeline or compromise on the quality of the exercise.

Let's bring back the game of soccer to understand one more situation. A very important entity in the game we have not talked about is the audience/fans. They come to the stadium by paying for a ticket to watch the game. Other than entertainment and the emotion of win/loss they do not get anything else. The team/owner will be ok in a scenario if the team loses a game but with full effort on the ground, wins the heart of the audience. The audience wants to see the commitment, effort, and passion of the team, and many times this impacts the decision of the owner. In the business world, to me, the audience is the society at large. People who may not get impacted directly, but still have an expectation from the organization. Most of the time, society expects businesses to be conscious of the impact they make on the environment, law and order, safety, security, well-being, convenience, etc. for the Public at large. There are many examples where big Industrial and Infrastructure projects are shelved because of people's resistance to the projects. Resistance may be due to their perception of possible negative impact on the environment, their livelihood, or health.

The idea behind talking about the above situations is to sensitize the readers that there are many important entities other than providers and customers who have the potential to disrupt the plans. These entities are called **interested parties** in ISO terms and **stakeholders** in regular business parlance. While customers remain at the core of all our plans and actions, the other stakeholders cannot be ignored. We need to consider the interests and requirements of these stakeholders, in order to be successful. For standardized approach, we can bifurcate the stakeholders under the following headings:

Stakeholder	Details
Customer	Customers are the most important stakeholders. The customer's customer and ultimate customer (end-user) also come under this group. Refer to Chapter 2 for further categories and subcategories.
Employees	This means people working in the provider's organization. For comprehensive coverage, human resources (people) deployed through other agencies on a contract basis should also be considered.
Partner/ Distributor	These are external entities who collaboratively work with us to meet the end goal. Partners bring their expertise and capabilities to the table which we might lack or do not want to develop in-house. In the case of distributors/agents/franchisees, they work like an extended team for us with mutual benefits.
Supplier/ Vendor	These are external entities who provide us with their product/service for which we pay them. We are a customer for them. In addition to direct supply, outsourcing orders for non-strategic works come under this category.

Continued...

Government/ Statutory Authorities	All law-making and governing bodies come under this group. They may be international, national, state, or local bodies. They formulate the rules of the game and expect everyone to follow them. The rules are introduced in the interest of the collective public good. Following the rules is not an option and is often mandatory.
Society	The public at large comes in this category. However, a more relevant section of society will be the group of people who are nearby our area of operations and get impacted, even slightly. Any impact on the environment, animals, flora, fauna, and natural resources including air, water, soil, etc. is considered an impact on society.
Owner / Shareholders	This is applicable in the case of bigger private organizations, where things are managed by professionals but ownership is either with a person/family. In the case of a public limited company, shareholders and the board of directors should be considered under this group.

As mentioned earlier, you need to consider the interests and requirements of these stakeholders in order to be successful. The same is to be done in the form of capturing applicable needs and expectations. The approach to understanding needs and expectations will be similar to what we went through for Customers under **Chapter 2 and Task 4.**

For employees, partners/distributors, and vendors/suppliers' formal feedback and satisfaction surveys are conducted by good companies. Similar to customer surveys, these surveys give good insights and areas of improvement. There are ways to understand the unarticulated needs of all stakeholders which I am not elaborating here.

Collated needs and expectations of all stakeholders are used for deciding overall and customer-specific strategic plans and projects. Successful organizations prepare stakeholder-based strategic plans and projects so that these stakeholders are also motivated to work with them. When their needs and expectations are fulfilled, they also win in their endeavors. When we practice our high focus on **customer's win with a cherished experience**, the stakeholders get positively influenced. They also start aligning themselves towards the ultimate customer. This impact on the stakeholders and the ecosystems is most desirable for us and the essence of **"winning together."**

To illustrate what can be the needs and expectations of different stakeholders, I am sharing an actual example from Godrej Construction. This is only for reference and one should gather the actual needs and expectations from respective stakeholders.

Key Stakeholders Needs & Expectations		
Stakeholder	**Key Needs & Expectations**	**Medium to Capture**
Business Stakeholders (BOD, CMD, President)	1. Predictable, Profitable & Sustainable Business Results (EBIT, EBITDA NBV, NOS, WC, ROCE) 2. Alignment with Company Purpose Vision Values 3. Compliance (Legal, Environmental, Health & Safety, etc.) 4. Enhance Brand Image	Annual Business Stakeholder Feedback, Monthly President's message, Annual strategy session, Quarterly reviews, Weekly meetings
Partners & Suppliers	1. Transparency in Dealings by Teams & Individuals. 2. Timely Payments & respect for Partners suppliers. 3. Collaboration for Improvement & adequate recognition 4. Business Growth Opportunities by strategic partnership.	Regular interactions with Business Head, Section Heads & Procurement Head, Get together, Vendor's & Partner's Meet, formal/informal meets and events, Vendor feedback survey, etc

Continued...

Chapter 8 Winning Together

Employees (People)	1. Healthy Work Environment & Work-life balance 2. Learning & Development (Focus on future emerging markets) 3. Growth Opportunities 4. Empowerment 5. Rewards, Recognitions, and Incentives	Employee Satisfaction Survey, HR representative/ Employee engagement task force, Management Committees, Weekly internal meetings, Town Hall meetings, etc
Society	1. Sustainable Development 2. Employment generation/ Skill Development 3. Social Impact of CSR Initiatives	Feedback during awareness programs, inputs from the parent organization, Need assessment survey, Program Evaluation Study, etc
Governing Stakeholders	1. Ensure Compliance (Legal, Environment, Health, Safety, etc.) 2. Payment of Dues 3. Support in Govt initiatives	Through Laws, Regulations, Acts, Guidelines, etc for Governing S/H.

Continued...

Customer - Real Estate Leasing	Trust & Transparency in transactions, Safe, Secure, and Hygienic workplace, Weatherproof structures, Client centricity, Assured Business Continuity, Scalability/ Affordability / Flexibility Options, Use of Technology & Automation	3rd party Satisfaction survey, Regular interactions, CRM meetings
Customer - Real Estate Development	Reliable and transparent dealings, Robust & Effective CRM, Meet commitments on Time & Quality, Future Ready Products, Best in class product offerings, Ease of Maintenance, Good Amenities	3rd party Satisfaction survey, Regular interactions, CRM meetings, Handing over feedback
Customer - Construction Material	Meet commitments on Time & Quality, Consistent quality, Customised concrete solutions, Single-point customer interface for concrete-related requirements, Value added products & Performance Based Concrete, Be Trustworthy Partner, Quick response & resolution of queries	3rd party Satisfaction survey, Regular interactions, Post pour Feedback

Task 17: Mapping Stakeholders Needs and Expectations

Referring to Chapter 2, Task 4, and the above example, readers to map the needs and expectations of all the relevant stakeholders. The collated information is to be used for strategy formulation. An alignment communication plan with or without the use of cascading will be prepared.

Task 18: Cascading Matrix

With the final strategy in place, readers to revisit the project list and map the required cascading afresh. Cascading matrix for measures to be prepared based on action cascading exercise. The key measure from the matrix will be used for regular status monitoring and performance evaluation of the team/person responsible.

Chapter 9

Conclusion

I want to tell you a short story written by the famous writer Mr. Kamlesh Tripathi to start with (Tripathi 2015) –

A long time ago there lived a man, who wanted to prosper in life, very fast. He went to a saint and expressed his desire. The saint smiled at him and gave him two coins, and asked him to drop the coins one after the other so that he could fulfill his desire.

The person felt extremely happy about his own sensible thought as his desire was soon to be accomplished. And before the saint could give him any other valuable advice, the person, while the saint was watching him, ran away from there.

After running a distance, and when he was out of his sight, he halted and dropped a coin to test. Just then, in front of him, and as he was watching, a golden chariot came and stood, and invited him for a ride. In the chariot, at

Chapter 9 Conclusion

a particular place, it was written 'Karma,' (which means action). Being excited and delighted, the young man sat in the chariot. And as he sat the chariot took to supersonic speed when the youth noticed there is no control lever in the chariot. For some time, he enjoyed the high speed of the chariot but soon he got nervous, as he was not sure about where he was going and his destination. He had no answers to his questions but the chariot was still moving at supersonic speed. He got scared.

When he was pondering about how to save himself from the high speed of the chariot, he saw a button on which it was written 'stop.' With great hope, he pressed the button. And immediately the chariot stopped. The person jumped out of the chariot and heaved a sigh of relief.

The journey had tired him. And after some rest when he was re-energized, with some renewed hope and strength he eagerly decided to drop the other coin, and as he did that another chariot came and stood in front of him on which it was written 'Akarma' (inaction) and it invited him for a ride. But this time the youth was less scared of the chariot when he entered.

But to his surprise this time the chariot was stationary, but around the chariot, everything was moving at a very fast pace and he was unable to see anything. And this moving of things at a fast pace started troubling him, and he felt giddy. When he could not withstand all this, to save himself he pressed the 'stop' button. The moving of everything around him stopped immediately. The person jumped from the chariot and ran towards the saint. He complained to the saint that by using the coins he has made no progress in his life.

The saint looked at him pensively, when he decided to explain and said, "Most people in the world want fast progress for themselves, and that too without any directional and sustained effort. While some are just the opposite. But neither hard work alone nor idling or inaction can give us progress." The saint further added, **"Every karma (action) of ours should have an objective. And there should be a particular procedure to do that karma (action) and there should be a continuous effort, and in this, factors that help are wisdom, intelligence, and sound ideas. And, when all these factors combine, then only we attain worldly and spiritual progress."**

This story conveys a message that karma (action) and akarma (inaction) both without an objective and continuous efforts are like a vehicle that does not have control levers for direction and control.

The message of the story is quite applicable to our efforts towards "Win With Your Customer." With a positive mindset, when we set a customer-focused purpose and vision, we are putting an objective in front of us. I have explained many approaches and systematic methods

Chapter 9 Conclusion

through which actions can be taken. The readers' tasks are designed with the aim that the learnings of this book can be implemented practically. I have tried to make this book like a worksheet to make the implementation easier. The strategy formulation flow chart under Chapter 8 gives a fair idea of the sequence of actions. But all these efforts will be effective only if readers initiate actions (karma) for themselves. If the book does not inspire the readers to take action for the success of customers and their own businesses, it has not met its main purpose.

The ideal scenario will be that you implement the approaches comprehensively with full faith in the process because all the topics discussed are interlinked. Still, if for some unavoidable reasons, it is not possible, start with smaller steps. Identify 1 or 2 areas from your business/profession that are most problematic. Go through the book again and see which approach seems to be a solution to your problem. Implement the approach (ideally with the help of a facilitator/expert) as a trial case. I am sure you will find some success. When you get initial success, do not let the momentum go down. Go back to the book again and again and find opportunities to implement balanced approaches.

An important point that should not be missed is about business context and environment. Today's business operating environment is considered to be VUCA (Volatile, Uncertain, Complex, Ambiguous). In fact, considering the post-pandemic era, there is more description like BANI (Brittle, Anxious, Non-linear, Incomprehensible). Technological transformations are happening in every area of life. In this scenario, organizations and professionals need to regularly relook at the customer-centric approaches they are adopting today. There may be a need to enhance the approach soon and we should be agile enough to take timely actions.

Finally, it is pertinent to quote the 'Golden Cycle of Continual Improvement' given by Mr. William Edwards Deming. **Plan-Do-Check-Act (PDCA).** For the execution of "Win With Your Customer," you must decide where you want to reach, set the quantifiable targets, identify the way to reach there, take along all the stakeholders, start taking actions as per plan, review the outcome of actions, take course corrections, understand and learn, improve the planning or make new plans, follow the cycle of PDCA for continual improvement.

"Winning With your Customer" is a journey where the process is more rewarding than the end. The most important action is to start the journey and stay on the path. I guarantee that this path is the road to success for you and all your stakeholders alike. My best wishes are to all the readers and their customers for their unlimited success. Signing off.

Readers' Tasks

For easy implementation of tasks provided under various chapters are reproduced here:

Task 1 (Chapter 2): Take a fresh notebook or an MS Office File (Word or PowerPoint) and use the same as your journal for all the tasks.

On top of the first page of the notebook write, "I believe and follow two Golden Rules."

After this write the golden rules I mentioned in Chapter 1 in a large font:

"Rule 1: The customer is always right!

Rule 2: If the customer is ever wrong, refer to rule number 1."

Task 2 (Chapter 2): Now, with your experience and explanation of the categories, please fill in the blank table provided under chapter 2 for your business or profession. While doing so you may, in addition, consider the product or service which you intend to launch in the future as well. Mark the categories or subcategories which directly influence the behavior of your customers or future customers as **primary (P).** Mark the categories or subcategories which may influence a few customers, or indirectly influence customer behavior as **secondary (S).** You can mark the remaining fields as **not applicable (NA).**

Task 3 Working table (Chapter 2): This task will be a continuation of the mapping you have done under task 2. Here, take each LoB/product one by one and identify the different customer groups under the applicable subcategories. The primary subcategories should be taken first.

Readers' Tasks

Task 4 (Chapter 2): From the task 3 table, you will take each **customer group** and identify their needs and expectations.

Task 5: Customer Feedback Survey (Chapter 3):

Readers will immediately decide on the plan for capturing customer feedback with or without a formal survey. The formal survey is to be designed with help of the steps provided in Chapter 3.

After going through all the chapters of this book, readers must relook at the plan they have prepared and enhance it if required. Once the final plan is in place, execute the same.

Task 6: Setting the direction and aligning with others (Chapter 4):

(A) If you already have a stated purpose and vision, please revisit your existing purpose & vision. Evaluate if they clearly indicate your preference to work towards making the customer a winner. If not, take a fresh look and recraft the purpose and vision.

(B) If you do not have a stated purpose and vision, you may have to take the help of a facilitator to conduct a proper workshop to arrive at a customer-focused purpose and vision.

Task 7: Identify value enhancement for customers (Chapter 4):

Sequentially, take each of the primary customer categories identified under tasks 2 and 3. For each of the primary categories of customers, you must follow steps 1 to 6 as per the flow and illustration that has been given under chapter 4.

The outcome of this task will be ideas for improvement or a new offering. After evaluating ideas and taking into consideration the efforts versus impact or cost versus benefits, you must take this ahead.

Task 8: Revalidate your process of customer feedback (Chapter 4):

The task is to evaluate and improve your post-feedback approaches. Please use points given under a) to h) and do the same for yourself.

Readers' Tasks

Task 9: Transform your customer communication plan as per learnings from Chapter 5.

(a) Map your customer journey under the 5 Stages (awareness, consideration, decision, retention, advocacy).
(b) Identify all possible touch points under the 5 stages and relook at the medium of communication.
(c) Use the principles explained—consistent messaging, updated in-sync communication, and listening to customers.

Task 10: Revalidate the customer complaint-handling process (Chapter 5):

Use the pointers given under (i) to (x) and improve.

Task 11: Identify the training needs of the team (Chapter 5):

Complete the mapping as per the sample shown and identify the required training modules for all.

Task 12: Actions to Enhance Customer Experience (Chapter 6):

In line with the illustrative table, identify the probable actions you can take for all the 5 stages customers go through. Think of yourself as a customer and be empathetic while doing this exercise. Also, try to incorporate pleasant surprises for customers to keep them interested. Relook at the customer engagement program as well.

Task 13: Study Customer Exit Analysis (Chapter 6):

See how you behave and treat customers when they exit. Evaluate if customers will be comfortable coming back to you if they wish to. Take the data from the last few years to understand why customers exited or did not buy from you. Do an appropriate analysis of data and see if some patterns or common reasons are appearing. If yes, those are the areas where you need to improve.

Task 14: Set a benchmarking process for yourself (Chapter 7):

Please use categories (Cat. 1 to Cat. 3) and benchmarking models (BM 0 to BM 3) to establish your own benchmarking process and implement the same. While you do the benchmarking, give special attention to the enabling technology being used by others.

Task 15: Identify relevant certifications or awards/competitions (Chapter 7):

Please go through the websites of ISO, CII, and respective industry/professional associations. Considering the best fit for your strategy and what your customers may find valuable, make the choice.

Task 16: Strategy Formulation and Supporting Project (Chapter 8):

The readers will relook into their existing practices and improve the same based on the flow chart I have created. The readers will implement at least one strategic goal through supporting projects immediately. Comprehensive changes can be made from the next year's strategy cycle.

Task 17: Mapping Stakeholders Needs and Expectations (Chapter 8):

Referring to Chapter 2, Task 4, and the provided in chapter 8, readers to map the needs and expectations of all the relevant stakeholders. The collated information is to be used for strategy formulation. An alignment communication plan with or without the use of cascading will be prepared.

Task 18: Cascading Matrix (Chapter 8):

With the final strategy in place, readers to revisit the project list and map the required cascading afresh. Cascading matrix for measures to be prepared based on action cascading exercise. The key measure from the matrix will be used for regular status monitoring and performance evaluation of the team/person responsible.

Answer to Quiz

A1: Complete the sentence - "If the customer is ever wrong, refer to Rule no.1 which is- Customer is always right"

A2: Right answer for customer categorization as (i) Kids (ii) Adults (iii) Senior Citizens - (a) Demography Based

A3: Need or Expectation? – "I just woke up; I need a cup of tea" – (a) Need

A4: Need or Expectation? – "Tea is not warm enough. Bring it in a neat and clean cup" – (b) Expectation

A5: The best way to understand customers' problems is to be sympathetic towards them. – (b) False. We need to be empathetic.

A6: One can get customer feedback by having a discussion with them. – (a) True

A7: Core for Setting Long-term Direction – (c) Purpose & (d) Vision

A8: Pain Reliever or Gain Creator?

    (i)   Pain Reliever

    (ii)   Gain Creator

    (iii)   Pain Reliever

    (iv)   Gain Creator

    (v)   Pain Reliever/Gain Creator depends on what problems/experiences users have in the current process

A9: Match the columns

Low Effort, High Value - Do Now

High Effort, High Value - Do Next

Low Effort, low Value - Do Later

High Effort, low Value - Don't Do

References

1. Customer-centric purposes of organizations from the Fortune 500 companies on Page 50 (Brand 2021) - https://purposebrand.com/blog/best-purpose-statements-fortune-500/
2. Examples of vision statements on Page 52 (Keenan 2022) - https://www.shopify.com/blog/vision-statement
3. Short Story on Page 160 (Tripathi 2015) https://kamleshsujata.blog/2015/07/08/short-story-karma-aur-akarma-action-and-inaction/

About Author

Devendra Dubey is a working professional in real estate and construction at a highly reputed, ethical and diversified business group in India. He is a practitioner of business improvement and transformation models such as EFQM (European Foundation for Quality Management), CII IQ Excellence Framework for Managing Customer Experience (developed in line with the customer-focussed requirements of internationally recognized excellence models) and ISO (International Organization for Standardization) for more than 12+ years.

He helped his organisation adopt these models into core business strategy planning and implementation. Being part of the core strategy group, he identified and implemented various initiatives which brought in customer focussed culture. While leading the customer focus group, he helped different lines of businesses improve their customer feedback and perceptions by taking the right actions. Better customer perception eventually led to better business for the organisation. Devendra was instrumental in getting various external awards for his organisation in varied fields like overall business, professional conduct, customer centricity, human resources, process management, best practices, etc., which has enhanced brand perception.

By education, Devendra is a civil engineering graduate with an additional degree in Law. Having an 'Executive Management Program' certification from the Indian Institute of Management, Calcutta (IIM C) and 'User Centric Innovation Design Program' certification from the Institute of Design, Illinois and Institute of Technology Chicago (ID Chicago), gives him a unique approach to challenge the status quo.

About Author

Born to a humble, ethical and reputed family in Dewas, Madhya Pradesh, he later moved to Mumbai, Maharashtra for his professional duties. He enjoys the company of his true friends and family and is a proud father of two sons Nabhya and Savya. By writing this book, his aim is to help create a society which works in complete harmony with high customer centricity.

www.ingramcontent.com/pod-product-compliance
Lightning Source LLC
LaVergne TN
LVHW041221080526
838199LV00082B/1343